RESUMES
that get you hired

RESUMES
that get you hired

● ● ● ● ●

Library of Congress Cataloging-in-Publication Data:

Resumes that get you hired.
p. cm.
Includes bibliographical references.
ISBN 1-57685-550-3
1. Résumés (Employment) 2. Job hunting. I. LearningExpress
(Organization). II. Title.
HF5383.R48 2006
650.14'2—dc22
2006000436

ISBN 1-57685-550-3

Printed in the United States of America

9 8 7 6 5 4 3 2 1

First Edition

For information or to place an order, contact LearningExpress at:

LearningExpress
55 Broadway
8th Floor
New York, NY 10006

Or visit us at:
www.learnatest.com

C O N T E N T S

RESUMES
that get you hired

INTRODUCTION

FINDING AND LANDING a new job can be an extremely time-consuming and stressful endeavor, especially if you're a recent graduate and making your way into the job market for the first time. Even if you're a successful professional looking for a new job, finding the job for which you're best suited will take time, energy, research, and all of the personal selling skills you can muster up in order to impress a potential employer.

Landing a new job is all about *sales*. Your primary objective is to sell yourself, your skills, education, work experience, personality, appearance, and motivation to an employer by using a variety of tools.

As a job seeker, your primary sales tool is yourself. When you are face to face with a potential employer in an interview situation, your ability to market yourself to the interviewer will determine whether or not you land a job. The employer will evaluate your appearance, personality, attitude, ability to communicate, how motivated you are, and, of course, whether or not you're qualified to fill the job for which you have applied.

Before you get to an interview, however, you need to attract an employer's attention using less personal means—your resume and cover letter. These documents communicate, in writing, your skills, accomplishments, professional background, and education. These tools can demonstrate to an employer that you communicate well in writing, and that you have the qualifications needed to fill the job opening.

Your resume and cover letter allow you to make either a positive or negative first impression. If you want to be invited for an interview, it's imperative that you make a positive first impression. To achieve this, your resume and cover letter need to capture the attention of the reader in less than ten to fifteen seconds. Simply by scanning your resume, someone should be able to determine who you are, your primary qualifications, what job you are looking to fill, and whether or not you have the core skills and experience necessary to fulfill the job's requirements.

Not only does your resume need to convey a lot of information in a relatively small amount of space, but every word, phrase, or sentence needs to convey something positive about you. Your resume must be well written, incorporate powerful words and phrases, and look professional. It should:

- Be easy to read
- Be well organized
- Be visually appealing
- Contain absolutely no grammatical or spelling errors
- Incorporate no negative information
- Include only information that's directly of interest to an employer

- Showcase information about you (your skills, work experience, accomplishments, education, etc.) in the most positive way possible

CREATING A RESUME: THE BASICS

Creating a resume that meets all of the aforementioned criteria isn't something you can create quickly. Plan on spending many hours gathering the appropriate information to be included, thinking carefully about how to present that information, choosing the best wording, and then actually writing your resume.

Chances are, between the time you start creating your resume and the time you actually send it to a potential employer, your resume will undergo many revisions and drafts.

Writing a powerful resume is a skill unto itself. If you're not comfortable with your own writing skills, consider hiring a professional resume writer or using one of the resume-creation software packages discussed later in this book (see Chapters 8 and 9). Although writing a powerful resume isn't an easy task, you *can* learn how to do it well.

As you'll soon discover, there are many different resume formats and types of resumes you can create. If you need a traditional printed resume, you can choose to follow a chronological, functional, or combination format; there's also a keyword-based resume format, which is becoming more popular as many employers currently use applicant-tracking software to evaluate resumes. As a job seeker, you will also need to determine if your resume should be scannable or if you need an electronic resume so you can easily apply for jobs online.

Any of these resume types can be created using a word processor or resume-creation software. These days, creating a resume using an old-fashioned typewriter is definitely passé and will be frowned upon by employers.

Although a resume may be a one-page document that you believe can be thrown together in a matter of minutes, it will actually take a lot longer if you want to set yourself apart from the competition, get noticed, and be considered for the best job opportunities. Your resume and cover letter need to make a positive impact on the reader, and most important, they must clearly communicate why you're qualified to fill the job.

One of the biggest mistakes job seekers make when creating their resume (aside from not proofreading the document and allowing spelling or grammatical mistakes to go unnoticed) is that they don't properly communicate their past employment history in terms the resume's reader will quickly and easily understand. Too many job seekers *undersell* their abilities or qualifications simply because they don't successfully communicate past work experience or describe previous job titles and responsibilities in an appropriate manner.

HOW THIS BOOK CAN HELP YOU

Resumes That Get You Hired will walk you through the entire resume process. By reading this book, you will:

- learn about the importance of your resume
- discover ways to add impact to your resume
- find out how to select the best format based on your personal situation
- learn how to put all of the pieces of a resume together into one powerful and well-written document
- discover how to choose effective wording that conveys important information
- learn how to avoid the most common resume mistakes
- find out about the many tools available that will make the resume process, and your whole job search process, easier and less stressful

This book also explores how you, as a job seeker, can use the Internet to help you find, apply for, and ultimately land a job; plus you will discover how to evaluate job opportunities and evaluate your own goals and objectives to ensure you find a job that's challenging, rewarding, and enjoyable.

To get the most out of this book, read it in its entirety. Then, go back and follow each step in the resume process, taking as much time as necessary to create your best possible resume.

KNOW WHAT YOU ARE LOOKING FOR

Far too many people get caught up in an employment situation that they hate simply because they're desperate to earn a paycheck. These people refused to do the necessary research and ask the appropriate questions before getting hired, and as a result, they wind up in a dead-end job, working with people they dislike. Once these people get involved in a bad employment situation, they often find it extremely difficult to pursue more rewarding career opportunities. Thus, they become frustrated and depressed, which negatively affects their professional and personal life.

Prior to accepting a position, you can do many things to determine if the job is being properly represented. By truly understanding your own skills and abilities, and knowing what your career goals are, you can better pinpoint job opportunities you will enjoy, and are qualified to fill. If you want to achieve long-term happiness and success in your industry of choice, it's imperative to find job opportunities that will provide a challenge and upward mobility. You will want a job for which you truly hold a passion.

Once you pinpoint that specific type of job, your resume and cover letter will play major roles in helping you land it. The key to success in every job search is preparation. Unfortunately, there are no shortcuts in the job-search process. You need to make the commitment to do the necessary research, track down the best job opportunities (using every method available to you), and then use your various sales tools (your resume, cover letter, thank-you notes, letters of recommendation, your personality, etc.) to do everything within your power to go after and land the best possible job.

To give yourself every possible advantage, don't hesitate to find a friend, mentor, career counselor, professional resume writer, former professor, or anyone else who can offer you assistance in finding job opportunities, writing your resume and cover letters, preparing for interviews, and ultimately succeeding in the whole job-search process. Also, be sure to use the Internet and take advantage of the online resources available to you.

No matter what type of job or career path you're pursuing, be persistent and don't settle for anything less than what you know in your heart you deserve. Finally, don't rely on any one tool or resource when it comes to finding and landing a job. Sure, your resume is extremely important, but it's only one of the tools of which you will need to take advantage in order to land a job.

Let this book guide you through the process of creating a powerful resume, but don't be afraid to let your own skills, personality, experience, and other marketable traits shine as you contact potential employers and seek out the best possible job opportunities.

APPLYING FOR THE RIGHT JOB FOR *YOU*

All too often, an applicant applies for what sounds like the ideal job, only to have his or her expectations shattered when the applicant discovers that the job advertisement was misleading or misrepresentative. No matter how well a job opening is described, it's *your* responsibility as the applicant to ask specific questions to avoid misunderstandings and to ensure that the job you accept is the one that you really want and for which you are truly qualified.

When applying for a job, you have several opportunities to learn as much as you can about the expectations of the employer and the actual responsibilities of the position. If you're responding to a help-wanted ad, one of the first things to ask a potential employer is to describe the job or to provide you with a detailed job description.

Advertisements that sound too good to be true probably are. If an ad is looking for, management trainees, that usually translates into an assistant retail store manager-type position, a commission-only sales job, or another low-paying sales position. The term *marketing of financial services* usually refers to some type of insurance sales, and ads that state *no sales* usually mean you will be selling something, either directly or indirectly. Companies recruiting people with a wide range of backgrounds for a specific job often look for as many candidates as possible for jobs that are not too exciting.

If you are invited to participate in a group interview with other applicants, a commission-only sales position is often being offered. If the employer evades questions about its product or service, or refers to extremely high income potential, that should definitely raise a red flag in your mind.

Accepting a job is like any kind of contract. You have to be clear about what you expect, and the employer has to be clear about what it's offering. As an applicant, you have to take an active role during the interview process and not always believe what people tell you. You have to ask questions. Having a slightly skeptical point of view can be helpful during the job-search process, but you can't come off as cynical or as an untrusting person.

Most of the time, companies that misrepresent job openings do so unintentionally. When discussing a job opportunity with a potential employer, you can't stay on the abstract level. Early on, ask what the specific responsibilities of the job are. If the interviewer uses descriptive phrases like, "work in a low-stress environment" or "flexible work hours," ask the interviewer to define exactly what that means. Often, how an employer defines terms in its job descriptions is different from how the applicant defines them. This leads to misunderstandings.

You need to ask questions like, "If I were to accept this job, what would you expect me to accomplish in the first three months and in the first year?" and "What kind of a person is successful working for your organization? What do they do, and what are they like?" As you ask these questions, urge the employer to provide complete answers about what will be expected of you.

PREPARING FOR AN INTERVIEW

Prior to an interview, prepare a list of at least five questions you can ask to help you better understand the position for which you are applying. Before accepting a job offer, ask if it would be possible for you to speak with people at the company who will be your colleagues. Some companies will be happy to grant you such access, especially as youy apply for higher-level positions. These potential coworkers will almost always tell you what to expect. They might not be able to explain things in bold or straightforward terms, but they will provide you with valuable information about what the job and the company. As you interact with potential colleagues, ask yourself if you would enjoy working with these people on a daily basis.

If the employer states that you will eventually be able to move up within the company, ask about training opportunities, how employees are evaluated, and how soon you could be considered for a promotion.

BEFORE YOU ACCEPT AN OFFER

Plenty of great jobs are available, but to find the position that's right for you, it's your responsibility to ask questions about the company and do plenty of research before accepting an offer. If you know what to expect, you can easily avoid unwanted surprises or landing in a dead-end or boring job.

As you turn the page, your job-search efforts are about to kick off as you begin to build an understanding of what a resume is and how you can best use this document to your advantage when applying for jobs. If used correctly, your resume can help you land the job you want, earn more money, and position you as a valuable asset to any employer.

RESUMES
that get you hired

CHAPTER 1

what a resume is
...and what it's not

SO, YOU'RE ABOUT to embark on a quest to land a new job. Perhaps you're looking to make more money, assume more responsibilities, or work for a new company. Maybe you're returning to the workforce after an extended absence, or you've recently graduated from high school, college, or graduate school and are entering the workforce for the first time. No matter what your reasons for beginning a new job search, finding the perfect job opportunity is going to take time, effort, and dedication.

The overall job-search process involves taking a close look at yourself, your education, skills, past work experience, overall qualifications, and marketability. You will need to determine what types of jobs or positions you're qualified to fill. Next, through research, reading help-wanted ads, networking, and surfing the Web, you will need to find job openings for which you're qualified.

Upon finding job openings, you will need to perform additional research to learn as much as possible about the potential employers and then submit a resume, cover letter, and/or an employment application to be considered for each position. Thus, your resume becomes an extremely important tool for marketing yourself to potential employers.

WHAT YOUR RESUME NEEDS TO DO

One of the most challenging tasks you will embark upon during your job-search process is writing a resume. After all, it will likely be the information on one single-sided sheet of 8½-by-11-inch sheet of paper that determines whether or not an employer invites you to an interview. On one sheet of paper, you have to concisely summarize, using examples, all of the reasons why a potential employer should hire you.

All potential employers that evaluate your resume will have a series of questions that they will want instant answers to as they read your resume. The primary goal of your resume is to answer the employer's questions quickly. When any human resources (HR) professional or potential employer reads your resume, your answers to the questions need to be obvious:

Exhibit 1.1. Questions Your Resume Should Answer about Your Qualifications

❏ Who are you?
❏ For what position are you applying?
❏ What are your skills and qualifications?

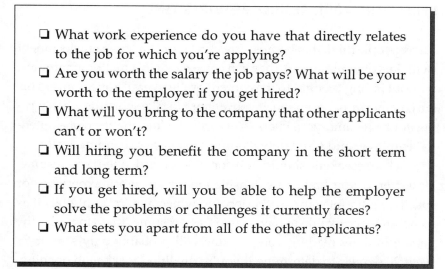

❏ What work experience do you have that directly relates to the job for which you're applying?

❏ Are you worth the salary the job pays? What will be your worth to the employer if you get hired?

❏ What will you bring to the company that other applicants can't or won't?

❏ Will hiring you benefit the company in the short term and long term?

❏ If you get hired, will you be able to help the employer solve the problems or challenges it currently faces?

❏ What sets you apart from all of the other applicants?

During a job interview, you must be prepared to answer all of these questions (and others) in detail. Your resume also needs to work as a sales tool and offer a preview of what an employer can expect from you now and in the future. Your resume has to be powerful, positive, attention getting, and 100% truthful.

When a potential employer reads your resume, it needs to shout out, "Hire me!" not "File me!" Writing a powerful resume is a challenging process that takes time, planning, much thought, and the willingness to make revisions until you have written what you believe to be the perfect document.

Anytime a company markets an expensive product, such as a major appliance, computer system, car, or some other type of machine, one of the first steps for enticing consumers is to provide a brochure that lists the product's unique benefits and features. The sales brochure is designed to get customers excited about the product before they actually see it firsthand. Similarly, when it comes to landing a job, your resume is the brochure you will use to market yourself. Your resume must get potential employers interested enough in you so that they invite you in for that all-important interview. From that point on, your chances of securing the job rely on your ability to sell yourself in person, but more on that later.

PERFECTING YOUR RESUME REQUIRES TIME

Many people think that because a resume is only a one-page document (with lots of white space), they can construct it in a matter of minutes, without giving thought to the content or the overall appearance. This is a common misconception. If you attempt to take shortcuts when writing your a resume, your chances of capturing the attention of a potential employer and ultimately landing a job decrease dramatically.

Most job seekers should rely on a standard one-page resume. However, if you have an extensive amount of work experience or specific skills relevant to the job for which you're applying, it is sometimes acceptable to have a two-page resume. Keep in mind, the person initially reading your resume will probably only scan it *for about 20 seconds* to determine if you're qualified for the job opening. All of the most pertinent information and key points you're attempting to convey should be attainable by *glancing* at the document for a brief period of time. If your resume is multiple pages, it becomes harder for someone scanning it to quickly develop an understanding of who you are and what qualifications you have.

Choosing what information to include in your resume, how to present that information, and finally, how you should customize your resume to target a specific job takes a lot of thought, creativity, and planning. Chances are, you will need to write, revise, and edit your resume multiple times before you create a document that you believe offers a preview of who you are and what you are capable of.

Writing a resume that makes a strong impact and that can effectively be used to market yourself to potential employers takes time and will probably require you to write and rewrite multiple drafts. If you want to experience success, it's critical that you make the commitment to yourself right now to invest as much time and energy as necessary to pursue every aspect of the job-search process correctly. You will have to have a good understanding of what a resume is, what needs to be included within it, and how to use it as a marketing tool. You must also understand how your resume is just part of an overall package you will soon present to potential employers.

Great Idea!

"Have extra copies of your resume ready, so that you can present a clean copy at your interview."

—LISA, ACCOUNT SUPERVISOR

THE ANATOMY OF A RESUME

No matter which resume format you use, the document itself gets divided into sections that make it easier to read and understand. As you read the next chapter of *Resumes That Get You Hired*, write down the pieces of information about yourself that fit into each resume section. Later, you will condense, organize, and rewrite this information, using action words to add impact.

Although not every resume includes all of these sections, the most common sections of a resume are:

- contact information
- job objective
- educational background
- employment experience
- professional affiliations
- military service (if applicable)
- personal and professional references

The rest of this chapter describes what you should include in each of these sections; Chapter 2 walks you through the process of compiling *your* information for each of these resume sections.

The Heading: Your Contact Information

At the very top of the resume, list your full name, address, phone number(s), and e-mail address. If you're still in school, include your permanent address as well as your school address.

If your job search is to be kept secret from your current employer, never list your current work phone or fax numbers, or your work e-mail address.

Whenever you list a phone number on your resume, always make sure that if a potential employer calls, the phone will be answered 24 hours a day. Make sure the caller can reach you on the first attempt. Connect an answering machine to the line, or subscribe to the call answering service offered by your local phone company. If a potential employer can't reach you easily, you could be passed over for a job.

The heading of a resume can be formatted in a variety of different ways, as long as the very first line of the resume (at the top of the page) lists your full name. Subsequent lines of your resume within the heading should explain exactly how to contact you.

Following are a few sample resume headings. Using your own creativity and personal taste, you can format your heading information as you see fit.

Heading Version #1

Full Name
Street Address
City, State, Zip
Home Phone Number
Cellular/Pager Number (optional)
Fax Phone Number (optional)
E-mail Address (optional, but strongly recommended)

Heading Version #2

Full Name, Street Address, City, State, Zip
Phone Number/E-mail Address

Heading Version #3

Full Name

Street Address
City, State, Zip
Phone Number
E-mail Address
Personal Website Address (optional)

Heading Version #4

Full Name

Street Address
City, State, Zip
Phone Number
E-mail Address

The heading information within your resume can be centered, right justified, or left justified as long as it appears on the top of the page.

Heading Version #5

Full Name

E-mail Address

Personal Website Address

Permanent Address	School Address
Street Address	Street Address
City, State, Zip	City, State, Zip
Phone Number	Phone Number

Job Objective

Okay, here's a challenge . . . In just one sentence, clearly state what position you hope to fill. To secure a job, the objective that you list on your resume should closely (if not perfectly) match the job for which you are applying. This sentence should be customized for each resume you send.

Don't write a generic job objective at the top of your resume, such as, Seeking a challenging and rewarding opportunity—this is worthless. It takes up space, but says nothing about you as an applicant. It also conveys to the employer that you don't know what type of job you're looking for, and you didn't want to take the few extra minutes necessary to customize and target your resume before submitting it.

When writing the job objective section of your resume, find the exact job title or description the company uses to describe the position available. This information is typically available within the ad or listing.

The heading you use for this section of your resume could be:

- Objective
- Position Desired
- Job Objective
- Employment Objective

- Job Target
- Goal

Suppose you find an ad that reads, "Executive Assistant . . . Seeking individual with strong communication and organizational skills; detail oriented, excellent writing and computer skills." For your resume's objective, you could write:

Objective: Seeking a full-time executive assistant position that would allow me to take advantage of my communication, writing, and computer skills.

Then, in the body of your cover letter, you could mention that you are extremely organized and detail oriented, which would refer back to the other requirements that were listed in the ad.

Describing Your Educational Background

Within this section of your resume, you will want to list your educational experience, starting with the most recent degree or certificate earned (or about to be earned). This includes your high school or college information, but it should also list any apprenticeship training, on-the-job-training, and accredited workshops or professional training courses you've completed. For example, if you're a certified Microsoft Office Specialist (see www.microsoft.com/learning/mcp/officespecialist/requirements.asp), you will want to mention when and where you completed this training.

Each item listed in this section of your resume should include the name of the educational institution you attended, the date of completion, the degree or certificate earned, and the city and state where the institution is located.

While listing each institution you attended, you can also include any courses or extracurricular programs you believe would be of direct interest to the potential employer. Listing your major is also essential.

On your resume, the heading you use for this section could be:

- Education
- Schools
- Academic Record
- Educational Background

....

If you're a recent graduate with an impressive GPA, this should be included with your educational background. If, however, your GPA isn't impressive and won't help to set you apart in a positive way, then it should be omitted.

....

Accreditation and Licenses

Any type of accreditation or license that directly applies to the job for which you're applying definitely should be added to your resume. This section can be used to showcase professional licenses you've earned in addition to, or in lieu of, a college degree. If you are currently in the process of earning a certificate or professional license, this should also be listed within this section of your resume, along with the expected completion date.

Some occupations require that, in addition to a traditional high school and/or college education, you also obtain some type of license, degree, or accreditation. For example, a real estate broker, notary public, lawyer, doctor, lifeguard, teacher, electrician, and plumber are all professions requiring special licenses, degrees, certifications, or accreditations. If you're applying for work in one of these fields, it's critical that your resume clearly states that you posses the necessary qualifications. Just as you include information about your educational background, you should list information about when and where you obtained your license, degree, certification, or accreditation.

Work or Employment Experience

Everyone has a collection of skills that make him or her better at a job. Some skills, such as computer literacy, are taught in school, whereas others are self-taught or are natural abilities. Spend a few minutes to create a list of the special skills you have that the potential employer might be interested in. Think about how each of the skills will make you do the job better. Also, list how you have successfully used each skill in the past.

Both on your resume and during an interview situation, be prepared to provide specific examples of how you have applied these skills. Certain skills, such as being bilingual or computer literate (with knowledge of specific software applications), are definitely worth listing on your resume.

Assuming you and the other applicants are qualified for the job, each applicant's personal skill set must set them apart from the competition and help an employer determine which person to hire. Within the Work/Employment Experience portion of your resume, the employment experience you list should be used to support the skills you have. This area of the resume can be used to demonstrate the real-world experience you have in using your skills.

Exhibit 1–2 is a short list containing examples of skill-related words you could list in your resume. See Appendix A for a more complete list of power words.

Exhibit 1–2. Action Verbs to Use on Your Resume

Analyzing…	Performing…
Coaching…	Planning…
Communicating…	Public Speaking
Consulting…	Record Keeping
Coordinating…	Researching…
Counseling…	Responsible for
Creating…	Scheduling…
Deadline Oriented	Selling…
Decision Making	Supervising…
Designing…	Teaching…
Developed	Telemarketing…
Innovating…	Training…
Motivating…	Web Content Creation…
Negotiating…	Web Page Design…
Organizing…	Writing…

sheet of paper, list all of your previous work experience, including internships, after-school jobs, summer jobs, part-time jobs, full-time jobs, and all volunteer or charitable work done to date.

As you add each entry to your list, determine the specific dates of your employment (month and year), and make notes concerning each position, your responsibilities, and your major accomplishments. Later, how you convey this information within your resume will be critical, so try to describe each experience concisely, using action words.

Great Idea!

"Look at your resume as a sales brochure: It's what you use to sell yourself to your potential employer. Make sure you list your most unique benefits and features."

—JUSTIN, TEAM LEADER

For now, write down anything and everything relevant about your work experience. When you create your resume, the heading you use for this section could be:

- Employment
- Job History
- Work Experience
- Professional Experience
- Employers
- Previous Employers
- Employment History
- Experience

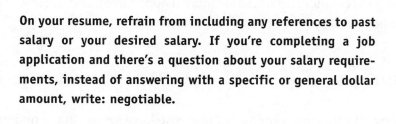

On your resume, refrain from including any references to past salary or your desired salary. If you're completing a job application and there's a question about your salary requirements, instead of answering with a specific or general dollar amount, write: negotiable.

When you are creating the Work/Employment Experience section of your resume, *never* include the reasons why you stopped working for an employer, switched jobs, or why you are currently looking for a new job.

Professional Affiliations

If you're a member of a professional group or association that directly relates to the job you're applying for, you should list this information on a section of your resume. Be sure to list any special involvement you have had or titles held within each organization.

Listing too many professional organizations, however, might cause a potential employer to become concerned that these obligations will interfere with your regular work schedule. Thus, choose one or two of the organizations to mention on your resume.

Participating in one or more professional associations provides an incredible networking tool for obtaining career-related advice, discovering unadvertised job openings, and obtaining introductions into various companies through the use of personal contacts.

When describing your professional affiliations, however, be sure to exclude any organizations that may be considered controversial. Leave out references to religious and political organizations, or organizations with whose philosophies not everyone agrees.

Keep the references short for the professional affiliations you do list on your resume. For example, list the name of the organization (the local chapter name and location, if applicable), and a few words about your involvement with the association.

Military Service

Many interviewers, especially those who have served in the military themselves, have a great respect for applicants who have served in the military and have been honorably discharged. The military is known for teaching skills like self-discipline and leadership, which all employers look for in applicants.

In addition to listing details about your military service on your resume, mention any specialized training you received while serving. Be sure to include when you served, your rank, and the branch in which you served. You should also mention any special skills you gained or decorations you earned while serving.

Personal/Professional References

If you are a new worker, your resume must fit on a single page. Thus, there's no need to waste valuable space listing actual references on your resume. You will have ample opportunity to share personal or professional references with a potential employer when completing an employment application and during your job interviews.

It is common practice, however, to include a line at the bottom of your resume that says: References available upon request. You should only add this if you have the space. Don't delete other useful information to make room for this statement.

Great Idea!

"Make sure to alert your references to the fact that they might be receiving calls from potential employers. Nothing's worse than an ambivalent or ill-prepared reference. You want to put your best foot forward and show the potential employer how great you really are!"

—CHRISTINE, CONTRACT REVIEWER

Adding Personal Information to Your Resume

As a job seeker, you are not legally obligated to disclose personal information, such as your age, sex, sexual orientation, race, marital status, family size, or handicaps; so whether or not you choose to include a personal information section on your resume is totally voluntary.

Whether or not you choose to discuss such information during a job interview is also your decision. Be aware that an employer cannot lawfully ask about any of these personal topics, and you are within your rights to refuse to discuss these matters with an interviewer.

Putting It All Together: Organizing and Prioritizing Your Information

Now that you've gathered and written down all of the raw information to potentially add to your resume, go through each piece of information on your pad and separate the items into categories based on where each will be included on your resume. For example, information that will go in the Work/Employment Experience section should be separated from information to be included in the Educational Background section.

Once you've organized each piece of information into sections, review your information and write the letter "A" or the number "1" next to the most important pieces of information. This is information you are certain needs to appear on your resume.

Continue by writing the letter "B" or the number "2" next to pieces of information that you would like to include on your resume but are not absolutely critical. When this is done, review your notes again, this time placing a "C" or the number "3" next to items that are less important but could convey information about you.

During the next review of your notes, write an "X" next to items that don't belong anywhere on your resume. These pieces of information may still be useful, for example, when writing your cover letters or preparing other materials to submit or discuss with a potential employer during an interview.

After you have prioritized each piece of information that needs to appear somewhere on your resume, you will need to rewrite the information to fit within the resume format you select. For a traditional resume, write consciously and use action words that add impact and emphasis to key points. At the same time, keep your sentences short (under 15 or 20 words each), and determine if bulleted points could communicate information more efficiently.

Great Idea!

"Don't wait until the last minute and throw your resume together. A good and effective resume takes time to assemble. Remember, your resume is your number one marketing tool; therefore, careful thought is the most important means to your success that you have at your disposal."

—CHRISTIE, HUMAN RELATIONS SPECIALIST

The rest of this book explains, in detail, how to take this gathered information and use it to create a great resume that showcases you as the best candidate for the job.

Now that you understand what a resume is, it's also important to understand *what it's not*. Your resume is just one of the tools used to land a new job. This document often provides you with your initial introduction to a potential employer (if you submit a resume in response to an ad, for example). When combined with a well-written cover letter, your resume package can help a potential employer make an educated judgment about whether or not it's worth the time to invite you for an interview to learn more about your skills, experience, and qualifications.

Your resume needs to convey professionalism; show you're an ambitious, hard, and dedicated worker; and also summarize your skills and qualifications. This document will offer an overview of who you are and provide the opportunity to proceed to the next step in the selection process.

Before an employer makes a job offer, you will probably have to:

- Submit a cover letter with your resume
- Provide recommendations from past employers and/or educators
- Complete an employment application
- Participate in one or more job interviews
- Write well-written thank-you notes after your in-person meetings with potential employers
- Pass a drug test (typically required only by very large companies or employers where drug use would be especially problematic, such as law enforcement or government)
- Have a background or credit check (at the employer's expense)

Your resume is just one of the things an employer considers when choosing whether or not to hire you, but it's extremely important.

Now that you know what type of information needs to be included on your resume, other chapters of this book will help you create a powerful and well-written resume that gets the attention of readers.

. . . .

The use of charts, graphs, and other graphic elements do not belong on a resume. Although these visual aids can be used during a job interview, the majority of the time, they're simply not appropriate for use in a job-search situation.

. . . .

WELCOME TO JOB SEEKING IN THE TWENTY-FIRST CENTURY

In the old days, when people were hired by a company, they were expected to remain employed by that company for their entire career, until retirement when they would receive a gold watch. Well, the days of gold watches are gone. These days, employees need to look out for themselves, while employers are constantly looking at the bottom line and consider new employees a financial investment and an impersonal commodity. Thus, during your career, you will probably change jobs and employers multiple times.

Thanks to technological advancements, upwards of 70% of all employers now use the Internet or applicant-tracking software for recruitment, which eliminates even more of the person-to-person contact between a company and an applicant during the hiring process. Applicants who understand how today's technology is being used by HR professionals and recruiters are certainly at an advantage.

compiling the necessary information to include on your resume

PUTTING TOGETHER AN awesome resume is an extremely important part of the overall job-search process. This short document needs to capture the attention of an employer quickly and then demonstrate, in no uncertain terms, that you're a qualified candidate for the job. Your resume needs to summarize who you are, what you know, what skills you have, what you've already accomplished professionally; list your career goals; and demonstrate why you should be hired.

Some people think a resume can be thrown together in a matter of minutes, because it's often only one page and typically uses bulleted points or sentence fragments. A resume is actually a rather complex document to create, however, because it has to convey key information in a limited amount of space. Anyone who doesn't invest the necessary time and energy to write an outstanding resume will most likely have a difficult time landing a job. When it comes to writing a resume, there are simply no shortcuts.

What a resume says is as important as how it's said and how the overall document looks from a visual standpoint. This chapter helps you determine what information you need to include in your resume. Later, once you know what needs to be said, this book will help you determine the best way to convey that information. Later chapters also help you choose the best resume format to meet your individual needs, select the best possible wording, and then format your resume so that it looks professional.

For now, don't worry about specific wording, resume format, or anything else. Simply focus on what information you believe needs to be conveyed within your resume. The following questions will help you summarize your skills, educational background, professional accomplishments, past work experience, career objectives, and other information you need to tell a potential employer.

Great Idea!

"Remember to ask yourself why your potential employer needs you specifically. What can you bring to the job that no one else can? Make sure to emphasize your best skills and accomplishments that come naturally and make you unique."

—JIM, CEO

Once you gather this information, you will later condense it, choose what's important, and decide the best way to convey it. As you answer the questions in this chapter, however, use complete sentences and spend whatever time is necessary to gather the specific information requested, such as dates or other pieces of information that will be pertinent later when actually creating your resume.

Be brutally honest with yourself as you respond to these questions. With accurate information, you will better determine what types of

job opportunities to pursue, evaluate the offers you receive, and ultimately choose the best career path to follow.

GATHERING YOUR INFORMATION

No matter what resume format you decide to adopt, the basic information included will be the same. As described in Chapter 1, typically, a resume includes the following sections:

- Contact Information
- Job Objectives
- Education
- Accreditations and Licenses
- Your Skills
- Previous Work and Employment Experience
- Professional Affiliations
- A History of Your Military Service (if applicable)
- Professional References
- Personal Information

The questions you're about to answer in the rest of this chapter
will help you determine what information to place within each of
these sections. If individual questions don't apply to you, skip them;
otherwise, include as much specific information as possible.

One of the worst mistakes you can make as a job applicant is
lying on your resume. These days, almost all employers check
resumes and references before offering someone a job. If an
employer discovers that you weren't 100% honest, the
chances that you will receive an offer are minute. Your resume
should be used to help you land jobs you're qualified for, not
as a tool to convey lies or misinformation to a potential
employer. Also, be forewarned that your new boss will expect
you to utilize all the skills you list on your resume. Wouldn't

it be more embarrassing if you couldn't perform the duties of your job?

Not only will completing this questionnaire help you create your resume, it will also help you prepare for your interviews and write your cover letters. You're about to summarize all of the reasons why a potential employer should hire you and identify reasons why it might not.

Great Idea!

"Don't neglect seemingly unrelated job experience. You can spin most skills into the skills required for the position you seek. For example, your skills as a babysitter require you to juggle multiple tasks at once, negotiate and settle tough and stubborn conflict, and manage your time effectively. These skills all make you an invaluable job candidate, no matter what job you are applying for!"
—Brenda, Teacher

Even if you ultimately choose to hire a professional resume writer or resume-preparation service to write your resume, you will have to supply the majority of this information. The same holds true if you purchase off-the-shelf resume-writing software for your computer.

CONTACT INFORMATION

Full Name:_____

Permanent Street Address: _____

City, State, Zip: _____

Daytime Telephone Number:_____

Evening Telephone Number: _____

Pager/Cell Phone Number (optional): _____

Fax Number (optional): _____

E-Mail Address (optional, but recommended): _____

Personal Website Address (optional) _____

School Address (if applicable)_____

_____

Your Phone Number at School (if applicable):_____

Although it's not necessary to include an e-mail address on a resume, it's strongly recommended for several reasons. First, it's often easier for a potential employer to contact you via e-mail. Second, listing an e-mail address on your resume demonstrates that you're computer literate, something most employers require. Listing a personal website also showcases your computer skills and provides potential employers with an additional way of learning more about you. Before releasing the URL, make sure your site or homepage is free of inappropriate or possibly damaging material.

If you don't yet have an e-mail address, consider joining one of the popular online services, such as America Online (www.aol.com), or signing up with a local Internet service provider. Many companies, such as Yahoo! (www.yahoo.com), Hotmail (www.hotmail.com), and Juno (www.juno.com), offer free personal and private e-mail accounts that can be accessed from any computer connected to the Internet.

JOB/CAREER OBJECTIVE

Write a short description of the job you're seeking. Be sure to include as much information as possible about how you can use your skills to the employer's benefit. Later, you will condense this answer into one short sentence.

_____

_____

_____

What is the job title you're looking to fill?_____

What are alternate job titles you're qualified to fill? _____

_____

EDUCATIONAL BACKGROUND

List the most recent college or university you've attended:

_____

City/State:_____

What year did you start?_____

Graduation month/year:_____

Degree(s) and/or award(s) earned:_____

Your major:_____

Your minor(s):_____

List some of your most impressive accomplishments, extracurricular

activities, club affiliations, etc.:_____

Grade point average (GPA): _____

Other college/university you've attended: _____

City/State:_____

What year did you start? _____

Graduation month/year: _____

Degree(s) and/or Award(s) Earned:_____

Your major:_____

Your minor(s):_____

List some of your most impressive accomplishments, extracurricular

activities, club affiliations, etc.: _____

Grade point average (GPA): _____

High school attended: _____

City/State:_____

Graduation date: _____

Grade point average (GPA): _____

Honors and awards received while in school: _____

_____

_____

List the names and phone numbers of one or two current or past professors, teachers, or guidance counselors you can contact about obtaining a letter of recommendation or list as a reference:

_____

_____

On your actual resume, you probably don't want to list your GPA or your class ranking, unless you graduated in the very top of your class. For now, however, include the information within this questionnaire. While in school, if you received any specific honors or awards, consider listing them within your resume, especially if they relate to the job for which you're applying.

PERSONAL SKILLS AND ABILITIES

Your personal skill set (the combination of skills you possess) is something that differentiates you from everyone else. Skills that are marketable in the workplace aren't always taught in school, however.

Your ability to manage people, stay cool under pressure, remain organized, use Internet resources or software applications (such as Microsoft Office), speak in public, communicate well in writing, communicate in multiple languages, or perform research are all examples of marketable skills.

Great Idea!

"When writing your resume, be sure to sell yourself—use phrases like responsible for, initiated, strategy execution, international, oversee. Your potential employers need to see that you are a really proactive person. Every employer wants someone who will take the initiative and get results."

—ANDREW, SALES DIRECTOR

When reading job descriptions or help-wanted ads, pay careful attention to the wording used to describe the employer's requirements. As you customize your resume for a specific employer, coordinate what the employer is looking for with your own qualifications as closely as possible. Try to use the wording provided by the employer within the ad or job description.

What do you believe is your most marketable skill? Why?

_____

_____

List three or four specific examples of how you have used this skill
in the past while at work. What was accomplished as a result?

1. _____

2. _____

3. _____

4. _____

What are keywords or buzzwords that can be used to describe your
skill? _____

_____

What is another one of your marketable skills? _____

_____

● ● ●

Provide at least three examples of how you've used this skill in the workplace:

1. _____

2. _____

3. _____

What unusual or unique skill(s) help distinguish you from other applicants applying for the same types of positions?

_____

_____

How have you already proven that this skill is useful in the workplace?

_____

_____

Be sure to list all of your marketable skills, whether you believe they're unique or not. For each of these skills, be prepared to describe how you've used them successfully in the workplace.

What computer skills do you possess?_____

_____

In what computer software packages are you proficient (such as Microsoft Office: Word, Excel, PowerPoint, etc.)? _____

_____

Thinking carefully, what skills do you believe you currently lack?

_____

What skills do you have that need to be polished or enhanced in order to make you a more appealing candidate? _____

_____

What options are available to you to either obtain or brush up on the skills you believe need improvement (e.g. evening/weekend classes at a college or university, adult education classes, seminars, books, home study courses, on-the-job-training, etc.)?

_____

_____

In what time frame could you realistically obtain this training?

_____

_____

WORK/EMPLOYMENT HISTORY

Most recent employer:_____

City/State: _____

Year you began work: _____

Year you stopped working
(write "Present" if still employed): _____

Job title: _____

Job description:_____

_____

Reason for leaving: _____

What were your three proudest accomplishments while holding this job?

1. _____

2. _____

3. _____

Contact person at the company who can provide a reference:

_____

Contact person's phone number: _____

Annual salary earned:_____

Employer: _____

City/State:_____

Year you began work: _____

Year you stopped working
(write "Present" if still employed): _____

Job title: _____

Job description:_____

_____

Reason for leaving: _____

What were your three proudest accomplishments while holding
this job?

1. _____

2. _____

3. _____

Contact person at the company who can provide a reference:

_____

Contact person's phone number: _____

Annual salary earned:_____

    Complete these employment-related questions for all of your pre-
vious employers, including part-time or summer jobs held while in
school, as well as temp jobs, internships, and volunteer work.

When it comes time to communicate with potential employers, you probably won't want to reveal your past earning history. You will want this information available to you for reference, however, when you begin negotiating your future salary, benefits, and overall compensation package.

MILITARY SERVICE (IF APPLICABLE)

Branch of service you served in: _____

Years served: _____

Highest rank achieved: _____

Decorations or awards earned: _____

Special skills or training you obtained: _____

_____

PROFESSIONAL ACCREDITATIONS AND LICENSES

List all professional accreditations or licenses you have earned. Highlight items that directly relate to the job for which you will be applying. _____

_____

_____

HOBBIES AND SPECIAL INTERESTS

List hobbies or special interests you have that are not necessarily work related, but that potentially could separate you from the competition, such as any competitive awards. Can any of the skills used in your hobby be adapted for the workplace? _____

_____

_____

_____

What non-professional clubs or organizations do you belong to or actively participate in? _____

_____

PERSONAL/PROFESSIONAL AMBITIONS

What are your long-term goals?

Personal: _____

_____

_____

Professional: _____

_____

Financial: _____

_____

_____

For your personal, professional, and then financial goals, what are five smaller, short-term goals you can work toward achieving right now that will help you ultimately achieve each of your long-term goals?

Short-Term Personal Goals

1. _____

2. _____

3. _____

4. _____

5. _____

Short-Term Professional Goals

1. _____

2. _____

3. _____

4. _____

5. _____

Short-Term Financial Goals

1. _____

2. _____

3. _____

4. _____

5. _____

Will the job(s) you will be applying for help you achieve your long-term goals and objectives? If yes, how? If no, why not?

_____

_____

_____

If you've answered "no" to this question, chances are you're pursuing the wrong types of jobs, or you don't yet have the qualifications needed to pursue the job opportunities you want. Think carefully about what you can do to remedy this situation. Also, don't be afraid to conuslt a career counselor who could help you narrow down your career focus and pinpoint your strengths.

Describe your current personal, professional, and financial situation.

_____

_____

_____

_____

What would you most like to improve about your life overall?

_____

_____

What are a few things you can do, starting immediately, to bring about positive changes in your personal, professional, or financial life?

_____

_____

_____

Where would you like to be personally, professionally, and financially five and ten years down the road? _____

_____

_____

What can you do to achieve these long-term goals or objectives?

_____

_____

_____

What are some of the qualities about yourself that you're most proud of? _____

_____

_____

What are some of the qualities about yourself that you believe need improvement? _____

_____

_____

_____

What do others like most about you? _____

_____

What do you think others like least about you? _____

_____

_____

If you decided to pursue additional education, what would you study and why? How would this help you professionally? _____

_____

_____

_____

If you had more free time, what would you spend it doing? _____

_____

_____

List the accomplishments in your personal and professional life of which you're most proud. Why did you choose these things?

1. _____

2. _____

3. _____

4. _____

5. _____

What were your strongest and favorite subjects in school? Is there a way to incorporate these interests into the job or career path you're pursuing? _____

_____

_____

What do you believe is your biggest weakness? Why wouldn't an employer hire you? _____

_____

_____

What would be the ideal atmosphere in which for you to work? Do you prefer a large corporate atmosphere, working at home, or working in a small office? If you're a recent graduate, think about what classroom environment in which you did best. _____

_____

_____

List five qualities about a new job that would make it the ideal employment opportunity for you.

1. _____

2. _____

3. _____

4. _____

5. _____

What did you like most about the last place you worked? _____

_____

What did you like least about the last place you worked? _____

_____

At what work-related tasks are you particularly astute? _____

_____

_____

What type of coworkers would you prefer to have? _____

_____

When it comes to work-related benefits and perks, what's most important to you? _____

_____

When you're recognized for doing a good job at work, how do you like to be rewarded? _____

_____

_____

_____

If you were to write a help-wanted ad describing your ideal dream job, what would the ad say? _____

_____

_____

_____

_____

_____

CONCLUSION

Only by carefully examining yourself, your objectives, your strengths, and your weaknesses will you ultimately find the best job opportunities; evaluate those opportunities; and choose the one that's best suited for you. When it comes to landing a new job, salary and compensation are important, but you also want to ensure you will be happy on the job and make sure you will be given the opportunity to move up the corporate ladder.

One of the worst mistakes job seekers make is not truly understanding what types of jobs they should apply for. As a result, they accept dead-end jobs, which make them miserable in the long term.

By pinpointing, in advance, your strengths and weaknesses and what types of jobs you're most qualified to fill, you will be able to write a resume that will be a powerful tool to help you land the perfect job.

Hopefully, by completing the questionnaire in this chapter, you've gathered vital information about yourself, some of which will soon be incorporated into your resume. By answering these questions, hopefully you started considering how you can best position and market yourself as an applicant and what types of job opportunities you're interested in pursuing.

In the next chapter, we will take the information you gathered by completing this questionnaire and begin creating your actual resume. The next major step in the resume-creation process is determining what resume format best suits your needs. For most people, a standard chronological resume format works well. However, if you're a recent graduate with little work experience, and large gaps in your employment history, or you're looking to change careers, one of the other popular resume formats may prove more useful.

choosing the
proper resume format

IN THE FIRST two chapters of this book, you learned about the various elements of a resume and completed a questionnaire designed to help you determine what information about yourself needs to be incorporated into your own resume. The next step in the resume-writing process is selecting a format. The format determines how you organize and display the information.

The resume format you choose should be based on several different criteria, including:

- Personal preference—When it comes down to it, you need to create a document you believe best showcases your skills, capabilities, and experience. Because your resume is being designed to promote you, it's only fitting that the format of the document be based partially on your personal taste. You will want to adhere to the main structure of whatever resume format you select, but there is room to add a touch of creativity. For example, Chapter 1 showed five different ways to lay out the heading (including centered, left justified, and right justified), which includes your name, address, phone number, and e-mail address (see pages 6–8).

- Your employment history—Depending on your personal circumstances, the format you choose can highlight your strengths while downplaying your weaknesses and any negative information in your employment history. Job searchers who have large gaps in their employment histories or who have jumped between jobs often should use a different resume format than someone who has a consistent employment history. Likewise, someone with little or no real-world work experience should create a resume using a different format than someone who has been working in the same industry for ten years.

- The job you're applying for—If you're applying for a traditional job at a small company, for example, you will probably want to use a printed resume, using a standard *chronological* format. If you're applying for a job at a dot-com or high-tech company, you will probably want to create an *electronic* resume and submit it via the Internet or e-mail. If a job at a large corporation seems more appealing, your resume will likely be scanned into applicant-tracking software and not initially read by a human. To prepare for this, you will want to create a *keyword-based* resume.

- The employer you're submitting your resume to— Employers typically have specific guidelines for resume submissions. For example, some only accept traditional printed resumes, whereas others prefer to receive an electronic file in a particular format (such as Microsoft Word,

Rich Text Format, or ASCII). When an employer states a defined resume submission policy, it's important for you to precisely adhere to that procedure in order to be considered for the job opening.

As you read this chapter, think about the types of jobs for which you will be applying, and determine which resume format best suits your needs. Keep in mind, it may be necessary to create several versions of your resume based on the type of job you're hoping to land. For example, you may want to have a traditional printed resume ready to submit to companies where you know an HR person (or executive) will be reading the resume, and also have a keyword version of your resume ready to send to companies using applicant-tracking software.

Once you have your basic resume completely written, modifying it to fit another format will be a far less time-consuming task, but one that could make the difference between receiving a job offer and having to continue your job search.

• •

To be the most competitive as an applicant, it's an excellent idea to create a traditional printed resume and then modify that resume into both a scannable (a resume that contains the same basic information as a traditional resume, but focuses on the use of keywords) and an electronic resume.

As the name suggests, an electronic (or digital) resume is not printed on paper. It's created on a computer, using a word processor, resume-creation software, or online resume form, then submitted to a potential employer using the Web (usually via e-mail). This way, no matter how a potential employer requests resumes to be submitted, you will be prepared.

• •

• • •

TRADITIONAL PRINTED RESUMES

Traditional resumes are printed on standard 8½-by-11-inch paper and are prepared using one of the resume formats described in this section. Until recently, this type of resume was by far the most popular. However, a growing number of employers (of all sizes and in all industries) are using computer technology to assist them with recruiting needs. Thus, some companies are taking advantage of applicant-tracking software and scanning resumes into a computerized database, and others have begun accepting resumes via e-mail or through one of the popular career-related websites. For companies that scan resumes or accept resumes electronically, a traditional printed resume isn't suitable.

A traditional printed resume is most suitable if:

- You're applying for a job at a small- to medium-size company that doesn't scan resumes into a computer database or use applicant-tracking software.
- You're attending a career fair and plan to distribute your resume to participating employers.
- You're meeting with an HR professional or recruiter in person.
- You're responding to a help-wanted ad or job posting that lists a mailing address as opposed to an e-mail address or website for submitting resumes.

The chronological resume format is the most popular. This format requires you to list your educational background and employment history in reverse chronological order (by date), starting with your most recent schooling and job. This format makes it easy for a potential employer who reads your resume to quickly see a summary of your qualifications. This resume format also allows you to demonstrate a progressive work history.

THE CHRONOLOGICAL RESUME FORMAT

The chronological format is the most popular out of all the different formats for traditional printed resumes because it's extremely easy for an employer to quickly see a summary of your work experience, skills, and education. The majority of job seekers use this format, especially those who have a consistent employment record and at least some work experience to showcase.

List your employment and education information in reverse chronological order. For example, in the Employment section of your resume, start with your most recent job or work experience, and go backwards in time as you progress down the page. Each past employer is listed separately, and each should include:

- Your dates of employment—When listing the dates of employment, use years only (1992–1996 or 1995 to Present). It's usually not necessary in your resume to list months you began or finished a job (June 1992–September 1996).
- Your job title
- The employer's name
- A brief listing of your primary accomplishments and the skills you used

Sample Format

Using the chronological resume format, Exhibit 3–1 is an example of what one of the listings might look like under the Employment section of your resume.

• • •

Exhibit 3–1. Sample Format of Employment Experience

Job Title   Employer's Name,
                                                  Employer's City, State

A short (one- or two-sentence) summary of your job and its responsibilities

- A bulleted item listing one specific achievement
- A second achievement
- Additional achievements, awards received, recognition received, promotions, etc.

Exhibit 3–2. Sample Listing of Employment Experience

EMPLOYMENT EXPERIENCE

IBM Corporation, Marketing Support Administrator
2005–Present

- Arrange, update, & schedule meetings via Outlook calendar on a daily basis for Marketing Director & Product Manager
- Process invoices (obtaining all necessary signatures) and update & track Excel invoice log daily
- Prepare expense reports for Marketing Director & Product Manager
- Was promoted from Administrative Assistant after only 6 months

For recent jobs, provide the most detail and information, especially when listing primary responsibilities and achievements.
Three to five bulleted items are appropriate. For less recent
jobs, include only two, or at most three, bulleted items for each.

The primary purpose of this resume format is to show you've
been steadily employed. It can demonstrate upward or lateral
mobility in your career path as you have moved from job to job.
Assuming you have work experience to properly use this resume
format, you will be able to demonstrate career direction. The job for
which you are curently applying should be the next step up from
your most recent work experience.

If you're a recent graduate, on the Employment section of your
resume, be sure to include part-time jobs, after-school jobs, internships, and volunteer work. This allows you to showcase whatever
real-world experience you have and highlight the work-related
skills employers will be interested in.

Great Idea!

"If you are using a recruiter in the industry where your
experience lies, always use the chronological format. It's
difficult to highlight your actual job experience in a
functional format. You might miss out on a wonderful
job opportunity if you don't seriously consider the format of your resume."

—Jennifer, Recruiter

Who It's Best Suited For

Applicants who have steady work and education records and can demonstrate constant growth or lateral movement with each position highlighted on their resumes will get the best responses when using a chronological resume. Job seekers with impressive job titles can easily demonstrate upward mobility and growth. Because this is the most popular resume format, most HR professionals prefer to receive it from applicants. Thus, if you choose a different resume format, you will want to make sure it highlights your strengths extremely well, because the person reading your resume will be curious as to why you *didn't* use a chronological format.

When to Avoid Using It

Although this is definitely a favored resume format among HR professionals, if you fall into one of the following categories, you should strongly consider using a format that better showcases your skills, capabilities, and potential, as opposed to your weaknesses. Don't use the chronological resume format if:

- You're a recent graduate with little or no work experience.
- You have large gaps in your employment history.
- You have negative information in your employment history.
- You're changing careers and have no experience working in the industry you're hoping to enter.

If there's only one gap in your employment history, you can still use a chronological resume format, but don't make it obvious that there was a period of time you were out of work. Never include a line within your resume stating, "Unemployed" or "Out of Work" along with the corresponding dates. For the time being, pretend it never happened.

Instead, focus on the positives—when you were employed and what you accomplished while employed. When asked about the gap, you could state that in between jobs, you took time off to pursue additional schooling, for example. However, if you have many small gaps in your employment history, strongly consider using a different resume format.

THE FUNCTIONAL RESUME FORMAT

This resume format organizes your past work experiences into functional categories. You use the same basic information as you would when preparing your resume using the chronological format, but instead of focusing on employment dates, the information listed in your resume will focus on your past job responsibilities and job titles. Using this resume format, you highlight your skills and give less prominence to your previous employers, employment dates, and job titles.

The functional resume format is best used by applicants who want potential employers to discover what they are capable of as opposed to when and where they've been employed. When using this resume format to showcase your skills and capabilities, you will be answering the question, "What specifically can you do for the employer?"

If you choose to create your resume using the functional resume format, select five or six of your most marketable skills that are applicable to the job for which you're applying. As you list each marketable skill, also include between one and three specific achievements from your past employment experiences that required use of that skill. You will also want to mention where you were employed when the skill was used.

A functional resume format begins with a heading and objective. Next, include a section that lists "Experience and Accomplishments." Within this section, list one of your skills at a time followed by two to four bulleted points describing what you achieved in the workplace using that skill. When describing your accomplishments, it's appropriate to mention the specific employer.

Great Idea!

"Make sure to use common resume headings, like Education and Experience. Your potential employer or HR representative might not notice your most marketable skills and experience if he doesn't recognize the headings you have chosen."

BOB, HUMAN RESOURCES REPRESENTATIVE

Sample Functional Resumes

Your items within this section of your resume might look something like Exhibit 3–3.

Exhibit 3–3. Sample Format for a Functional Resume

Experience and Accomplishments

Your Most Marketable Skill That's Directly Related to the Job for Which You're Applying
- Your biggest accomplishment using that skill, followed by the employer
- Another accomplishment using that skill

Your Second-Most Marketable Skill
- Your biggest accomplishment using that skill, followed by the employer
- Another accomplishment using that skill

Below the Experience and Accomplishments section, a summary of your employment history should be featured. Format this section in reverse chronological order, as shown in Exhibit 3–4.

Exhibit 3–4. How to List Your Employment History on a Functional Resume

Professional Experience or **Employment History**

| 20##–Present | Job Title/Position | Employer |
| 20##–20## | Job Title/Position | Employer |

Exhibit 3–5 shows an actual example of a functional resume, in part.

Exhibit 3–5. Sample Functional Resume (partial)

EXPERIENCE AND ACCOMPLISHMENTS

- CONCEIVED and PRESENTED customized analytics designed to assess Asset Liability Management risk profiles, which led to increased sales of securities to banks, credit unions, and municipalities.

- DESIGNED and MANAGED a fee-based financial planning system incorporating investment, fringe benefits, business continuation, and estate planning.

- DIRECTED and MOTIVATED a young and inexperienced salesforce to achieve record-breaking sales growth over a two-year period in the most competitive marketplace in the country.

EMPLOYMENT HISTORY

Charles Schwab & Company, Investment Specialist II	2001–Present
Clinical Diagnostic Services, District Sales Manager	1999–2001
SmithKline Beecham Clinical Laboratories, Senior Territory Sales Manager	1996–1999

Who It's Best Suited For

For job seekers whose career path thus far doesn't fit nicely into a chronological resume format, the functional resume format is probably the next best thing to use. This resume format works best for:

- Recent graduates with little or no real-world work experience
- People with large or multiple gaps in their employment history
- Highly trained job seekers who have little actual work experience
- Job seekers with extensive unpaid volunteer work experience
- Job seekers with non-work-related experience that helped them develop skills that will be useful in the workplace
- People who are changing careers and will be working in a different industry, which was the reason behind the sample resume shown in Exhibit 3–5.

When to Avoid Using It

Most HR professionals prefer to see chronological resumes, because this format allows them to evaluate someone's entire career path in a matter of seconds. When an applicant doesn't use a chronological format, the reader might assume the applicant is trying to hide something about his or her past. When reading a functional resume, it's harder for a potential employer to put together an applicant's employment history or career path. To compensate for these potential drawbacks, it's critical that the information included on your functional resume be extremely relevant to the reader and to the job.

THE COMBINATION/TARGET RESUME FORMAT

If you pinpoint a specific job opportunity with a specific company and you want to create a customized resume specifically for that potential employer, you might consider using this resume format. All of the information included within this type of resume is used to support the statement, "I am the perfect applicant for this job, because..." Use this resume format if you already know the exact requirements and skills the job requires. When using this resume format, focus on why you're qualified to meet the job's requirements based on the skills you already have.

Using a targeted resume format allows you to combine elements of the chronological and functional formats. When listing your employment history (in reverse chronological order), the focus will be on showcasing your most marketable skills. The dates of employment, however, can be tucked away at the end of each employment listing, so it takes the emphasis away from any gaps in your employment history.

Sample Combination Resumes

Using the combination/target resume format, Exhibit 3–6 is an example of what one of the listings might look like under the Employment section of your resume.

Exhibit 3–6. Sample Combination/Target Resume

Job Title Held, Top Skill Used   Employer's Name

Short description of your most marketable skill (one sentence)
- Work-related accomplishment that involved using this skill
- A second work-related accomplishment that involved using this skill

Short description of another marketable skill of interest to a potential employer
- Work-related accomplishment that involved using this skill
- A second work-related accomplishment that involved using this skill

(Employment Dates) 20##–20##

Who It's Best Suited For

This format works well for applicants who know exactly what job they want and who understand the exact job requirements of a position. Thus, your resume can be custom tailored to the employer's requirements. This type of resume also works well for someone who posseses the skills needed to fill a specific job, but doesn't have related work experience.

When to Avoid Using It

Because this resume is targeted for a specific position with a specific employer, the main drawback to this format is that if you're not offered the job you want (because the employer doesn't think you're qualified, for example), you might not be considered for similar opportunities from that employer.

Great Idea!

"When looking at a resume, what I first notice is a consistency in resume format. I look at the order the candidate lists his skills, make sure the fonts are consistent, and check that the way he lists his education and experience is consistent. An inconsistent format signals an inconsistent worker who isn't detail oriented."

—Carli, Project Coordinator

BIOGRAPHICAL RESUME FORMAT

Someone who is applying for a non-traditional job and is extremely accomplished in his or her field might use a biographical resume.

This resume format is typically one page long, however, it lists someone's accomplishments using several paragraphs of text (composed of complete sentences as opposed to bulleted points). Because the applicant is submitting a full page of text, this format takes longer for someone to read and pinpoint pertinent information. Nevertheless, if you're already highly respected in your industry and have extensive experience, this resume format is useful. When submitting a resume is more of a formality than a requirement when applying for a job, this is the resume format to use.

When printing a biographical-style resume, use 8½-by-11-inch paper, and an easily readable font (such as Times Roman) printed in a 12-point size. To make the document easier to read, consider using line-and-a-half spacing and taking advantage of 1¼-inch left and right margins, as well as 1-inch top and bottom margins.

At the top of this resume, include your basic heading information (full name, address, phone numbers, e-mail address, etc.). This should be followed by one or two paragraphs listing your most recent achievements. Continue describing your professional accomplishments and employment experience in reverse chronological order. Thus, details about your educational background are listed toward the bottom of the page.

In terms of popularity, this style of resume isn't too common, so by submitting it to a potential employer, chances are you will stand out. Unless you have extremely impressive credentials, you should not use this resume format.

If you read other resume books or speak with resume-writing experts, some recommend using alternative, but less popular, resume formats. The linear, accomplishment, professional, and academic curriculum vitae resume formats are among the others you might read and hear about.

Although you want to stand out from the other applicants, it's important to provide HR professionals or recruiters with the information they desire and need—in the format they're used to receiving it. Thus, although you should incorporate some of your own creativity into the design of your resume, it's an excellent strategy to stick with a popular and widely accepted resume format.

ELECTRONIC RESUMES

An electronic or digital resume is one that will be e-mailed to a potential employer, posted on a career-related website, or included within an online resume database. Some employers that accept electronic resumes have a specific pre-defined resume form on the company website that must be completed online to be accepted. This also holds true for the majority of career-related websites.

Other employers that accept electronic resumes request that the documents be created and saved in a specific file format, such as Microsoft Word, Rich Text Format, or ASCII. When creating an electronic resume, adhere exactly to the formatting specifications provided by the employer or career-related website.

Instead of following the same format as a traditional printed resume, use keywords as opposed to action verbs to describe your employment history, skills, and education. For more information about how to create an electronic resume and how to take full advantage of today's computer technology and cyberspace when searching for a job, see Chapter 7.

> **To use an electronic resume, you must have access to the Web as well as your own e-mail account. If you don't own your own computer, you can find connected computers at a public library, a college/university, an Internet café, or by visiting a friend or relative who owns a computer. It is not advisable to use the Web access or e-mail address at your current place of employment for your job search.**

Who It's Best Suited For

Anyone applying for jobs online must have an electronic resume. This includes people using any of the career-related websites or those plannig to apply for a job directly through a company's website. Electronic resumes are also ideal for sending via e-mail. The majority of large companies currently accept electronic resume submissions.

When to Avoid Using It

If you're applying for a traditional job that requires a traditional printed resume.

SCANNABLE/KEYWORD RESUMES

One of the fastest growing trends among medium- and large-size companies is to incorporate applicant-tracking software into their HR practices. Applicant-tracking software allows an employer to create a list of keywords for each job opening. These keywords are used to describe the job's requirements, the necessary skills, and the educational background for the ideal applicant. Once this list of keywords is created by the employer, the software allows employers to take traditional printed resumes or electronic resumes and automatically scan or import them into a database without someone reading or evaluating them.

Once an applicant's resume is entered into the database, the software deciphers it, word by word, and compares each word to the listing of keywords created by the employer. Only those applicants who have resumes with a pre-defined number of keyword matches will be flagged as potentially qualified applicants for a job opening. After the software has selected the top candidates, an HR professional can read only those applicants' resumes or interview those people.

As a job seeker, if you will be applying for jobs at medium- to large-size companies that already use applicant-tracking software, it's important to create a resume that will be compatible with applicant-tracking software. Focus on using keywords within your resume that you believe will match keywords the employer has already selected. Instead of using action verbs (as you would for a traditional printed resume), incorporate *nouns* that describe your skills, experience, and education.

Although a scannable or keyword-based resume can follow any of the formats of a traditional printed resume, the wording will be different. After the heading section, some applicants add a section called "Keywords," which is simply a listing of nouns, phrases, industry terminology, and buzzwords you know the computer will search for when it evaluates your resume.

Although you're creating a printed resume you believe will be read by a computer, you should still follow the resume design tips provided in this book for traditional printed resumes. After all, there's always a chance someone might look at your resume, and you want them to be impressed.

When you create your resume on a computer, using a word processor or resume-creation software, save that document file, just as you would any other document. A traditional resume (one that is to be printed and then sent to potential employers), which you save on your computer's hard disk as a Microsoft Word document, for example, is different from an electronic (digital) resume that will be formatted differently, will take advantage of keywords, and will ultimately be e-mailed (not printed on paper and sent) to a potential employer.

In today's cut-throat business world, it's extremely common for a job seeker to have multiple versions of his or her resume. It's definitely a worthwhile time investment to take your traditional printed resume and modify it into a scannable resume.

When printing and formatting a scannable resume that will be submitted to an employer in hardcopy form, follow the specifications listed in Exhibit 3–7.

Exhibit 3–7. Guidelines for Formatting a Scannable Resume

- Use white paper with black ink.
- Use a standard font that's easily readable by a computer scanner.
- Don't use underlining, bold, or italic text.
- Use simple formatting—no lines, boxes, columns, or other graphic elements. Also don't use the following symbols: #, %, &, or hollow bullets that might not be readable by the scanner.
- When using a dash "–", you can either leave space between the words or numbers where the dash is being placed or delete the space on both sides. Whichever you choose, make sure you are consistent. For example, 2000 – 2005 or 2000–2005.

- Don't fold or staple the resume.
- Make sure the ink is dark and easily readable. If the resume can't easily be scanned into the employer's computer system, or if it scans improperly because the ink is too light or smudged, the computer won't recognize those all-important keywords (even if you're totally qualified for the job), and you will get passed over.
- Within the text of your resume, avoid using abbreviations—spell everything out.
- Use a laser printer (as opposed to an inkjet, dot matrix, or daisy wheel printer) to print a document you know is going to be scanned.
- Make sure your full name is the first piece of information, located at the top of the page. The rest of the resume's heading information should follow, but place your e-mail address on a separate line.

Don't make the assumption that the company you will be sending your resume to isn't high-tech enough to use applicant-tracking software.

Who It's Best Suited For
Anyone applying for a job at a medium- to large-size company in any industry that uses applicant-tracking software should take advantage of this type of resume. If an employer uses this type of software, the job ad may indicate it.

When to Avoid Using It

If you're a top-level executive who knows your resume will be read and evaluated by a person rather than a computer, creating an electronic or keyword resume won't be useful or necessary. Likewise, if you're absolutely sure your resume will be read and evaluated by a person, focus on creating a traditional printed resume as opposed to an electronic resume. People applying for jobs at small companies probably don't need this type of resume.

putting your resume together

BY NOW, YOU should have a pretty good idea of what type of job you're going to be applying for, and hopefully you have spent ample time evaluating yourself to determine what makes you marketable in today's competitive business world. You should also have identified major similarities between the job openings and your qualifications.

By completing the questionnaire in Chapter 2, you have already gathered the information to incorporate into your resume. As you read Chapter 3, you should have selected the resume format that fits your personal needs.

The next step in the resume-writing process is to take all of this information and put it together into what will become your resume. This chapter will help you:

- Format your resume content so it fits the selected resume style (chronological, functional, targeted, etc.).
- Develop the best way to state each piece of information within each section of your resume.
- Decide whether or not to use bulleted lists within the various resume sections.
- Select the best action verbs and power phrases to add impact and ultimately sell yourself to a potential employer.

BETTER RESUME, BETTER OFFER

Unless you're currently employed and looking for a new job on the side, the fact that you're unemployed is costing you money in lost wages. Obviously, the sooner you land a new job, the faster you will begin receiving a paycheck. By creating a powerful resume, not only will you land a job faster, but your resume can also be used to position you to earn a higher salary in the future. You can represent yourself as someone with higher earning potential through the way you use job titles and define your skills and expertise on your resume.

If you receive a job offer from an employer, the salary offered will be based on how the employer values you, and that will be based on your resume and your interview. When an employer offers you a job and then proposes a salary or compensation package, that offer will be based mainly on the employer's bottom line—not on how much an employer likes you as a person.

Every employer typically has a salary range to offer someone filling a specific position within his or her organization. The low and high ends of this range can be several thousands of dollars apart. Additionally, there are various negotiable benefits. Based on your educational background, proven skills, and work history, an employer decides how much of an asset you can be to his or her organization and determines where your salary should fall within the predetermined range.

If the employer thinks you're simply qualified to fulfill the responsibilities of the job, you will be offered a salary that's on the lower end of the range. In the future, you may receive raises once you've proven your skills, but you will start out earning less money than you would had you proved yourself a more valuable candidate early on, both on paper and in person.

If you're perceived to be more than qualified, because you have proven skills the employer wants, plus you're able to demonstrate your ability to quickly take on additional responsibilities, the employer will value you more. As a result, your chances of being offered a salary that's on the high side of the range is much more likely.

One of the roles of your resume, once it captures the employer's attention, is to showcase you as a valuable asset to whomever you will work for. As someone reads your resume, he or she should easily see how your skills and experience can be immediately put to good use within his or her organization.

MAKING YOUR RESUME'S CONTENT FIT THE FORMAT YOU CHOOSE

The resume format you choose should be based on a variety of criteria. Most important, choose a format that allows you to showcase your skills, education, and work experience in the best possible light. Once you've selected your resume format, review each piece of information you believe should be on your resume and determine where it belongs.

Great Idea!

"Don't forget to use both a spell checker and a proofreader. A person can catch errors your computer's spell checker can overlook, like the difference between *it's* and *its*. In addition, it is especially helpful to have someone read your resume to you out loud. That way, you can make sure it reads the way you want it to."

—Wes, Risk Manager

As you begin to formulate the look and contents of your resume, consider the following examples to determine how the information should be presented. No matter what resume format you choose, each piece of information needs to be conveyed using the fewest possible words and in the most exciting and impressive way.

Exhibits 4–1 and 4–2 are two sample resume formats available to you as a job seeker. The first is the most widely used—the chronological format, and the second is an alternative—the functional, which you might use instead in order to focus on your skills as opposed to your employment history. As you look over these sample resume formats, think about how you will plug in your own information.

• • •

Exhibit 4–1. Sample Chronological Resume Format

Your Full Name
Street Address, City, State, Zip
Phone Number/Cellular Number
E-mail Address

Objective: A one- or two-sentence summary of your accomplishments and your career objective. This should be specifically targeted to the job for which you're applying.

Work Experience

20##–Present   **Your Job Title**   Employer
A one-sentence description of your responsibilities.

- Using three to five bullet points, include short, concisely written accomplishments, listed individually. Use specific facts and figures to support your statements.
- List a second accomplishment.
- List a third accomplishment.
- List a fourth accomplishment. Since this is your most recent job, include more information about it. For subsequent jobs, list fewer points. Be sure to list specific skills you used to succeed.

20##–Present   **Your Job Title**   Employer
A one-sentence description of your responsibilities.

- Using two to four bullet points, include short, concisely written accomplishments, listed individually. Use specific facts and figures to support your statements.
- List a second accomplishment.

Education
School Name (City, State)
Major, GPA, Highest Degree Earned, Graduation Date

(List each school separately, and include all degrees, honors, credentials, and licenses earned.)

Exhibit 4–2. Sample Functional Resume Format

Your Full Name
Street Address, City, State, Zip
Phone, Fax, E-mail

Objective/Job Title You're Pursuing
In one or two sentences, explain your specific career goal(s), or convey to the reader what job title you're looking to fill and why you're qualified.

Experience
List Your Most Marketable Skill (It must relate directly to the job you're pursuing.)
- List your most impressive achievement using that skill, followed by the name of the employer and the employer's city and state.
- List a second achievement you've accomplished using that skill thus far in your professional career and the employer information.
- List a third achievement and the employer information. Since this is your most marketable skill—the biggest reason why you should be hired, use up to five bullet points.

List Your Second-Most Marketable Skill
- Include up to three bullets describing how you've used this skill thus far in your career. Each bullet should include one example and list the name of the employer, plus the employer's city and state.
- List another example of how you've used this skill successfully.

List Your Third-Most Marketable Skill
- Include up to three bullets describing how you've used this skill thus far in your career. Each bullet should include one example and list the name of the employer, plus the employer's city and state.
- List another example of how you've used this skill successfully.

Provide Another Reason Why You're Qualified for the Job
- List up to three or four achievements, areas of proficiency, specific skills, etc. (using separate bullets) that the employer will find impressive.

Employment History

19##–Present	Job Title	Employer's Name
19##–19##	Job Title	Employer's Name
(List each employer)		

Education
Include degrees earned, the educational institution(s), graduation dates, etc.

MAKING YOUR INFORMATION STAND OUT

Within five to ten seconds, the person reading your resume must be able to determine who you are, what job you're applying for, and why you're qualified to fill that position. If your resume doesn't achieve this objective, it needs to be revised.

To capture the attention of the reader, no matter what resume format you're using, you need to make each piece of information sound important and somehow related to the job for which you're applying.

Great Idea!

"Bulleted lists are easy on the eye. They highlight each important piece of information in your resume."

—GRETA, SALES DIRECTOR

Stating Your Objective

Your resume's objective needs to convey, in no uncertain terms, a synopsis of your accomplishments, skills, and any other favorable information that will help convince the reader to keep reading. The most common mistakes people make when creating their objective statement, for example, is brevity or stating something that's generic or obvious.

Weak Example

The following statement is too generic and does nothing to showcase the applicant's abilities. Thus, it does nothing to sell or promote the applicant.

Objective: To work in a Public Relations position offering advancement opportunities.

Because you want to state what position you're applying for and include at least one or two reasons why you should be considered as an applicant, a better way to use this space is to state:

Objective: To work as a Senior Account Executive at a public relations firm that would allow me to use my eight years' experience developing PR campaigns, writing press releases, working with corporate clients, and interacting with major media outlets.

Some people use an objective statement within their resume to state the job for which they're applying. An alternative is to use a summary statement, which describes your qualifications in a short sentence. For targeted resumes, however, it's ideal to use an objective statement that incorporates elements of a summary statement, provided you can do this concisely.

Describing Your Work Experience

When you're ready to begin writing the work experience section of your resume, for a traditional printed resume, begin each sentence, bulleted point, or item of information with an *action verb*. Appendix A offers an extensive list of words and phrases you can incorporate into this section of your resume.

For each item of your resume, use a different action verb. Avoid being repetitive or redundant. For example, find alternate ways of stating information if you held similar positions with different employers.

Writing in a style that's concise yet punchy is a skill. To convey the information in this section of your resume, plan on writing and then rewriting your text many times. To help you make your accomplishments sound better, for each job title you've held, ask yourself the questions listed in Exhibit 4–3.

Exhibit 4–3. Questions to Ask Yourself When Describing Your Work Experience on Your Resume

❏ What was your job title? Be specific.
❏ Does the job title sound generic? Will someone immediately be able to determine what the job title means?
❏ What were your top three responsibilities?
❏ What specific actions did you take to accomplish your job-related responsibilities?
❏ What problems did you face while on the job? How did you overcome them?
❏ What skills did you use in the job? How did you use them? What was the result?
❏ What are some action verbs and keywords you can use to describe your job, its responsibilities, and your accomplishments?
❏ Is there a better way to word your job titles, without lying, to make them more descriptive or sound more impressive?

As you piece together answers to the preceding questions, check a newspaper's help-wanted section or go online and find five or more ads for positions that are similar to the one for which you're applying. Study the wording of these ads and choose keywords that you can incorporate into your resume to describe job titles, responsibilities, experience, etc. If you understand exactly what the employer needs, your goal is to explain, using your resume, how your experience makes you qualified to meet the responsibilities of the job.

Even though you're looking at several different ads, perhaps published by different employers, if the openings are for similar positions, chances are the job requirements and desired applicant qualifications will be similar. Thus, by evaluating multiple ads, you can create a list of the employer's requirements and then determine how your personal qualifications allow you to meet those job requirements. This is information that you need to highlight on your resume.

As you assemble this information, focus on providing as much specific information as possible. If you're writing about your skills as an administrative assistant, for example, in addition to listing your typing speed and accuracy, list specific word processing programs you're proficient in using, such as Microsoft Word, WordPerfect, and so forth.

Each of the job titles you use to describe past work experience will also have an impact on the reader. For example, listing a past position as *Administrative Assistant* signifies you're probably capable of doing tasks like answering phones, typing, and filing. If the person reading your resume sees job titles like *Office Manager* or *Executive Assistant*, it's implied that you've taken on additional responsibilities and can be of greater value.

Although you may think of yourself as an administrative assistant, one of your responsibilities while working for your last employer might have included booking travel itineraries (business trips) for the executives within your company. Under your Executive Assistant job title on your resume, listing one of your responsibilities as "travel coordinator" is a perfect example of how you can use your resume to highlight skills and responsibilities a potential employer will find useful.

When describing each of your skills, you want to highlight information that makes you more marketable. For example, if one of your skills is working as a typist, you should include the skill "Word Processor—proficient in Microsoft Office applications, including Microsoft Word" in your resume.

If you're using a chronological resume format, simply by looking at your job titles, the reader should be able to see career advancement. Because your most recent work experience will be listed first, your highest job title should be the one described first. So, if that job title was Marketing Manager, for example, other job titles listed on your resume (as the readers work their way back in your employment history) might include Assistant Marketing Manager, Marketing Associate, and Marketing Intern. With each item, you should be able to demonstrate career advancement. If you can't, consider using another format, such as the functional resume.

Appendix B at the end of this book discusses how to best use job titles to enhance your resume, make yourself stand out, and position yourself as someone with higher earning potential than equally qualified candidates who don't sell themselves properly using their resumes.

Simply listing impressive job titles along with a series of related skills isn't enough. It's also important to provide examples of *how* you achieved success in your past jobs, using specific examples. For example, using statements with specific dollar or numeric figures often adds impact to your statements.

For example, an experienced Marketing Director might make statements such as "Managed the company's $30 million marketing budget," "Trained the company's ten-person marketing staff," and "Launched three of the company's most successful products in 2005." These are impressive statements that demonstrate skill, leadership ability, and a strong knowledge of product marketing. Each statement opened with an action verb, such as *managed*, *trained*, or *launched*, and included a specific fact, such as a $30 million budget, the size of the team, and so forth. You should do the same on your resume, making the most of your skills and abilities, even if you don't yet have this impressive work experience.

It's important to use action verbs to describe your accomplishments, skills, and so forth, but it's easy to use big words that can make you sound pretentious. Whenever you can use a simple word that has impact as opposed to an obscure one, always keep your resume easy to read.

After listing each job title and employer in the Employment section of your resume, devise one or two full sentences of text, followed by bulleted points that support that sentence. Using action verbs and short sentences allows you to convey the maximum amount of information in the shortest possible space. As you write, make sure the voice and tense of the text remains consistent.

One common mistake made by many job seekers is they list their current job's employment dates as "20##–Present," and although they are still employed, they describe their current employment using the past tense. Likewise, people creating a resume tend to switch between first and third person within the text.

Weak Example

Using bulleted points as opposed to paragraphs makes it much easier for someone reading your resume to quickly determine what information you're trying to convey. For example, within your resume you could write:

1993–1998   **Sales Manager**   **The ABC Company**

Responsible for managing a sales team of 13 people and developing the sales tools used to sell the company's products. During the 5 years of my employment, sales increased an average of 15% per year. The company's products were also introduced into new retail outlets. As a result, distribution for the company's products expanded by 50%. In 1998, under my supervision as project manager, an e-commerce website was launched, allowing the company to sell its products online.

The preceding paragraph lists several extremely important points that an applicant would want a reader to notice. The problem is, if the person responsible for reading your resume only glimpses at it for less than 20 seconds, he or she won't carefully read the paragraphs of text you worked so hard to incorporate into your resume.

Better Example

A better way to present this information is to use bulleted points, with each point starting with an action verb or power phrase designed to capture the reader's attention. Using the same information in the previous example, here's a better way to present the facts using bulleted points in a standard chronological resume. Never try to incorporate too much information into a paragraph, sentence, or bulleted item.

1993–1998   Sales Manager   The ABC Company

Managed and trained a sales staff of 13 people. Developed and implemented all sales tools currently used by the company.

- Responsible for a 15% increase in sales per year.
- Coordinated sales efforts targeting new retail outlets, resulting in a 50% increase in retail distribution.
- Developed and implemented an e-commerce website, allowing the company to accept orders and promote its products online. The site receives 250,000 hits per week from current and prospective customers.

As you create drafts of your resume, add as many bulleted items as necessary to convey what you believe is the most important information about each of your employment experiences. When you begin to edit your resume, you can prioritize, condense, and delete items that aren't absolutely necessary.

Your bulleted items need not be complete sentences (as long as they make sense, of course). If you're using a paragraph style, you must use complete, grammatically correct sentences. Under no circumstances are spelling mistakes or typos acceptable.

Education

Place the Education section of your resume toward the bottom of the page. Just as you listed your employment history or the university you attended in reverse chronological order, you should first list your most recent degree earned.

When listing a college diploma and some form of graduate degree, there's little need to include information about your high school. If you haven't attended graduate school, however, include your highest level of education completed (or that you're about to complete, listing your anticipated graduation date).

CONCLUSION

This chapter has walked you through the basics of putting your resume together:

- what information your resume should include
- how you should format it (remember: you might also choose to use a functional resume, but the chronological format is usually preferred)
- how to state yor objective effectively
- how to describe your work experience thoroughly
- how to describe your education

To bring this all together, Exhibit 4–4 is a sample chronological resume that illustrates all of the advice and suggestions in this chapter. The next chapter focuses on other formatting issues to ensure that your resume is easy to read by HR managers and hiring managers.

Exhibit 4–4. Sample Chronological Resume

Henrietta P. Lee

Current Address: 34 East 59th Street, 4D • New York, NY 11111
                                            212-555-9974
Permanent Address: 8754 West 72nd Street • New York, NY 11111
                                            212-555-3559

EXPERIENCE:

(7/05–Present)   **Blinker's Institutional Research**
Junior Equity Research Analyst
Analyze medical device companies for independent equity research firm specializing in emerging medical technologies. Perform technology assessment and financial valuation through financial projection, technical analysis, field research, and company SEC filings. Responsible for writing research reports targeted for institutional investors. Give verbal consultations as part of service to clients and subscribers of the retail product—a weekly medical investment letter—covering over twenty medtech and biotechnology companies.

(5/03–6/05)   **Johnson's Pain Relief Medical Services**
Medical Assistant/Office Manager
Assisted in procedures with pain patients to relieve and manage their symptoms. Handled medical billing, managerial, and medical administrative tasks. Managed follow-up issues, including payment recovery from insurance companies and preparing letters to the Office of the Attorney General to render past due payment. Used extensive communication and writing skills.

(5/04–6/05)   **John S. Graham Memorial Cancer Center**
Research Assistant to Neal Blake, MD, Chief of Pain Service
Executed pancreatic cancer study, specializing in the relief of cancer pain. Performed research in medical journals and through MEDLINE. Other duties included data abstraction, data collection, and results analysis.

(9/02–12/02)	**East River HIV Center**
	Clinical Research Assistant/Data Analyst
	Abstracted and recorded relevant data to the HIV prevention study from patient medical records.
HONORS:	**Columbia College Dean's List** 2001–2005
	Joel Jackson Scholarship 2002–2003, 2003–2004
ACTIVITIES:	Columbia College Academic Awards Committee
	Judge 2004–2005
	Columbia College Woman's Mentoring Network
	Mentor 2004–2005
	Columbia College Admissions
	Tour Guide 2003–2005
	New Student Orientation Program
	Advisor 2003–2005
SKILLS:	Microsoft Office, Lotus 1-2-3
	Native Mandarin Chinese Speaker
	Proficient in French and Latin
EDUCATION:	**Columbia University**
	Bachelor of Arts, History and premedical studies, May 2005

Note: Because the page size of this book is smaller than the standard 8½ x 11" resume page, this sample is set as two pages. Your resume should be only *one page*.

CHAPTER 5

your resume's appearance: make sure it's easy to read

EVERY ELEMENT AND section on your resume is important. This sheet of paper needs to convey all of the information a potential employer needs to make an educated decision about whether or not you're qualified enough to invite for an interview. Because of your resume's importance, it's imperative to spend considerable time developing the content, so that every word, line, and section makes a positive impact on the reader. Not only should your resume pique the reader's interest, it should excite him or her about the prospect of meeting you in person.

No matter how good the content, however, it won't make a bit of difference if an employer is turned off by your resume's appearance, and chooses to skip it in favor of a better looking one on the pile. The first impression your resume makes is critical. It should be visually pleasing to the eye, printed on high-quality paper, coordinated with your cover letter and envelope, and not look intimidating.

It doesn't matter which resume format you decide to adopt (chronological, functional, targeted, etc.). When creating a traditional printed resume, how the document appears on the page is the first thing a reader notices.

If you don't believe you have the creativity and taste necessary to create a visually appealing document, study as many sample resumes as possible, paying careful attention to layouts, fonts, line spacing, margins, and other visual elements.

This chapter explains many of the design elements you need to consider when creating your resume. As previously mentioned, make sure your entire resume package (your resume, cover letter, personal business card, envelope, etc.) are all coordinated and work together for a greater overall visual effect. Using the same paper type and color, font, ink color, and design elements for each of these documents helps you convey the fact that you're well organized, detail oriented, and able to communicate well in writing.

CHOOSING THE BEST RESUME PAPER

When you are creating your resume and cover letter, how these documents look and feel are as important as what they say. When applying for most jobs, you want your cover letter and resume to convey a highly professional and somewhat conservative image. To achieve this, you will have to choose the right paper, select the right resume format, and decide whether or not to add a touch of color in order to make your resume stand out. Resumes that stand out in a positive way are the ones HR professionals and recruiters read first.

When you visit an office-supply store or print shop to purchase resume paper, you will be surprised at how many different shades of white there are. You will also find paper stocks in several different weights and textures, some containing watermarks, and most will have at least some cotton content.

The most traditional choices for paper color are bright white, ultra white, or ivory. The paper colors in the white family ensure the text on the page will be legible (depending, of course, on the font, typestyles, and ink color you choose). Resumes printed on white paper are also better for scanning, which helps eliminate the possibility of applicant-tracking software misreading something on the page.

For traditional printed resumes, it's also acceptable to use a slate or light gray paper. Avoid using bright-colored or dark-colored papers, however, which will cause your resume to stand out for the wrong reasons. As for the weight of the paper, 24- or 28-pound bond paper works fine. One way to help your resume stand out is to use a heavier paper stock. Expect to pay between $.15 and $1.00 per sheet for quality resume paper unless you buy a box of 50–500 sheets at an office-supply store.

....

Warning: Don't try to fold a resume that's printed on a heavy paper stock (over 28-pound basis weight) in order to insert it into a business-size envelope. If you're using a heavier paper stock for a resume package, send it in a large (9 by 12-inch) envelope.

....

Make sure the paper color and ink color work well together to maximize readability. The ink color you choose for your resume and cover letters should be standard black. Navy or burgundy are also acceptable. Some people choose to use a small amount of different colored text (a second color) within their resume to highlight specific items. This strategy can be effective, but using multiple colors is not considered traditional. Multicolor printing is also more expensive if you're using a professional printing service, and using a color inkjet printer doesn't usually offer the print quality needed for a resume. Unless the multicolor print quality of your resume looks totally professional, use one ink: traditional black.

According to the director of marketing at Paper Direct, "You want your resume to stand out, but you also want your documents to look professional and be easily readable. Sometimes that's a contradiction. No matter what type of paper and ink color you select, it's vital that your resume, cover letters, thank-you notes, and envelopes all match. Part of being professional is being coordinated."

The job you're pursuing and the industry you hope to work in should also determine the look of your resume. Graphic artists should show creativity through the use of graphics, design, and color in their resume package, whereas someone applying for a traditional job in the business world should stick to the basics in terms of traditional resume layout and design.

When choosing resume paper, make sure you see and feel a sample of the paper stock prior to purchasing a sealed package of that paper. Finally, when printing your resumes and cover letters on a laser or high-quality ink-jet printer, make sure the paper you choose was designed for this equipment.

Instead of racing to your local office-supply superstore and grabbing the first package of paper you find suitable for your resume, shop around a bit. Visit a local print shop or copy shop and look at all of the different types of available paper. As long as you select a resume paper that conveys a professional image, the actual paper you choose is a matter of personal preference.

Great Idea!

"Avoid paper that is too loud or outrageous. Although I am always looking for someone with energy and creativity, fluorescent green paper screams flashy, inelegant, and egotistical to me! It also detracts from the actual content of the resume. Who can concentrate on a candidate's skills when you can't stop looking at the paper?"
—MARGARET, HUMAN RESOURCES EXECUTIVE

•　•　•

Make sure your resume package forms a presentation that you're pleased with and can be proud to show and distribute to potential employers. Remember, the appearance of your resume package says a lot about you and will most likely play a major role in creating a positive (or negative) first impression with an employer.

Resume Paper Selection Do's and Don'ts

- Don't use generic, 20-pound, white bond paper that's typically used with photocopy machines and laser printers.
- Do select paper with at least 50% cotton content and a basis weight of between 24 and 28 pounds.
- Do keep in mind when selecting a paper color, bright white or ultra white are the most traditional shades of white used for resumes and cover letters. Ivory, slate blue, or gray papers are acceptable alternatives.
- Don't overspend. Papers that contain a watermark can add a touch of formality to your resume package, but these papers typically cost more and don't add a huge amount of impact to your resume's appearance. Using paper with a watermark is a matter of personal taste.
- Do use a dark ink, such as black, blue, or burgundy, when printing your resume package. Incorporating a second color ink, such as red, can also be used sparingly to highlight key points in your documents. Keep in mind, however, that using two ink colors on a resume is not considered traditional. If you're having your resume professionally printed, using multiple colors gets costly.
- Do ask for a sample before ordering paper for your resume and cover letters from a mail order or Internet-based company. When placing your order, include matching envelopes and matching note cards (for your thank-you notes), so that everything looks consistent.

SELECTING FONTS, TYPE SIZE, MARGINS, AND INK COLOR

When creating a resume to be read, you have a bit more freedom in terms of the font(s), type sizes, and ink colors to choose than if you're creating a resume you know is going to be scanned. (See the last section of this chapter for tips on how to create a scannable resume.)

Choosing a Font

For readable resumes, after you've created the content, and you know which resume format you will be following, choose a font that is easily read and pleasing to the eye. Once you select your font, stick with it. Use only that one font on your resume. Mixing and matching fonts makes your resume package look cluttered and unprofessional. Some of the most popular fonts for resumes include:

- Times Roman
- Palatino
- Ariel
- Garamond
- Century Schoolbook

Upon choosing one of these basic and easy-to-read fonts, you also have access to a variety of typestyles that can be used to capture the reader's attention. You want to use different typestyles sparingly and only to highlight specific pieces of information. Boldface, small capitals, underlined, and italic type can be used effectively.

Exhibit 5–1 shows a few examples of standard styles you can choose from when creating your resume package.

Exhibit 5-1. Samples of Standard Resume Fonts

This is an example of Times Roman—Normal type.
This is an example of Times Roman—Bold type.
This is an example of Times Roman—Italic type.
This is an example of Times Roman—Underlined type.
You can also mix and match typestyles, using ***bold and italics together***, or **bold and underlining together**, for example.

This is an example of Palatino—Normal type.
This is an example of Palatino—Bold type.
This is an example of Palatino—Italic type.
This is an example of Palatino—Underlined type.
You can also mix and match typestyles, using ***bold and italics together***, or **bold and underlining** together, for example.

This is an example of Ariel—Normal type.
This is an example of Ariel—Bold type.
This is an example of Ariel—Italic type.
This is an example of Ariel—Underlined type.
You can also mix and match typestyles, using ***bold and italics together***, or **bold and underlining** together, for example.

This is an example of Garamond—Normal type.
This is an example of Garamond—Bold type.
This is an example of Garamond—Italic type.
This is an example of Garamond—Underlined type.
You can also mix and match typestyles, using ***bold and italics together***, or **bold and underlining** together, for example.

This is an example of Century Schoolbook—Normal type.
This is an example of Century Schoolbook—Bold type.

> *This is an example of Century Schoolbook—Italic type.*
> This is an example of Century Schoolbook—Underlined type.
> You can also mix and match typestyles, using ***bold and
> italics together***, or **<u>bold and underlining together</u>**,
> for example.

As you can see from Exhibit 5–1, when you have a paragraph or series of bulleted points that use too many different typestyles, it looks extremely unprofessional and busy on the page. However, highlighting a single word in a sentence with bold or italics, for example, can add impact.

Choosing a Type Size

Based on how much information you need to fit on a page, you can select the font size that's most appropriate. Font sizes are measured in points. Most people use a 12-point font when printing their resume. If you need to fit more text on a page, however, you can use a smaller, 10-point type, or if you don't have enough information to fill the page, you can use 13-point type.

Within your actual document, refrain from mixing type sizes. When using 12-point type, use it for the entire document. Also, avoid using a type size that's too small or too large. Don't go any smaller than 10-point type or any larger than 13-point type. If your resume is printed using a font that's too small, it will be difficult to read. Likewise, if the font is too large, your resume will appear unprofessional and childish.

Exhibit 5–2 shows how different type sizes look on the printed page:

Exhibit 5–2. Examples of Different Type Sizes

- This is 9-point Times Roman Normal.
- This is 10-point Times Roman Normal.
- This is 11-point Times Roman Normal.
- This is 12-point Times Roman Normal (the ideal type size for a resume).
- This is 13-point Times Roman Normal.
- This is 14-point Times Roman Normal.

Adjusting the Margins

When using resume-writing software or the Resume Wizard built into recent versions of Microsoft Word (see Chapter 8 for details), the margins of the page will automatically be set for you to accommodate the text on the page. The margins are the white space around the edges of the printed page.

If you are manually creating your resume on a word processor, however, it's your responsibility to set the margins on the page. For example, with Microsoft Word, you can easily adjust (and modify) the margins of a document by selecting the Page Setup, then Margins option under the File pull-down menu. When using most word processors, you can adjust the top, bottom, left, and right margins. As a general rule, you will want to set the margins as follows for an 8½-by-11-inch page:

- Top   1"
- Bottom   1"
- Left   1.25"
- Right   1.25"

- Gutter   0"
- Header   .5"
- Footer   .5"

Your resume should be no longer than a single page, especially if you are starting out in your career. If you have a lot of information to include, keep in mind that you can adjust these margins slightly to help fit your resume to a page—for example, you could reduce the left- and right-hand margins to only an inch. But don't get *too* creative: If there's no white space left on the page, your resume will be difficult to read, so make sure you're not changing margins to accommodate information that isn't necessary to include. Edit first; then reformat.

Great Idea!

"Make sure your resume looks clean, polished, and balanced. Your resume is a potential employer's first view of you. You want to make sure that you reveal yourself in the best manner possible."

—Nicholas, Public Relations Specialist

Choosing an Ink Color

As mentioned, black ink on white paper is the most common traditional printed resume. You can stray from this rule by using a dark blue (navy) or burgundy ink color. If you choose to incorporate an ink color other than black, and you do it tastefully, you could wind up with a resume package that grabs the reader's attention in an extremely positive way.

Should you choose to incorporate colored ink or papers, it's an excellent strategy to work with a resume-preparation specialist or a graphic designer to ensure your selections will have the most positive impact possible. Using ink and paper colors that clash make you look foolish and unprofessional, and they could keep the *content* of your resume from getting read.

Printing Your Resume Using a Computer

Using virtually any computer that's connected to a printer, you can create and then print resumes using a word processor or resume-writing software. When printing your resume and cover letters, however, be sure to use the highest quality printer possible. It is *not acceptable* to use a dot matrix printer or an older ink jet printer, because the resolution and quality of these devices isn't high enough, in most cases, to generate a professional looking document. Ideally, you will want to use a 300dpi, 600dpi (dots per inch), or better laser printer for generating your resume and cover letters.

If you own a computer, but no laser printer, you can create your document using any word processor and then save the files to a disk. You can then visit any Kinko's, CopyMax, or other printing company, and for a fee, have your files printed on a high-quality printer directly from your disk.

MAKING YOUR RESUME SCANNABLE

A scannable resume is a printed resume that is scanned and evaluated by a computer as opposed to being read by someone. You will have to modify the resume's content and appearance for the scanner.

The biggest rule to follow when creating a scannable resume is to create the content by using *nouns* and *keywords* in the text as opposed to action verbs. When it comes to actually printing your resume, consider the requirements of the computer system being used by the potential employer to which you will be sending your resume.

When a resume is scanned into applicant-tracking software, it's put through a scanner, which takes the entire document and converts it into digital form. The software then picks apart the resume, word for word, looking for specific keywords and phrases. For this process to work, the scanner must be able to read your resume clearly. Thus, it's important to format your resume and print it in a way that helps eliminate the possibility of computer error.

Information about formatting your resume so that it's compatible with computer scanners and applicant-tracking software was offered in Chapter 3. Some of the key formatting points included:

- Use only white paper with black ink.
- Use a standard font that's easily readable by a computer scanner.
- Don't use underlined, bold, or italic text.
- Use simple formatting—no lines, boxes, columns, or other graphic elements. Also don't use the following symbols: #, %, &, or hollow bullets that might not be readable by the scanner.
- Make sure the ink is dark and easily readable.
- Use a laser printer (as opposed to an inkjet printer, dot matrix printer, or a typewriter) to print any document you know is going to be scanned.

Throughout this book, you've read about the importance of using action verbs in a traditional resume to add excitement and impact as you describe your skills, educational background, and work experience. However, when creating a resume that will be scanned, adding excitement to your resume does little good, because the computer software that will evaluate your resume (to determine if it's worthy of being read by someone in the company's HR department) will only be looking for a specific set of keywords and phrases. A list of keywords (see Exhibit 5–3), and a sample scannable resume (Exhibit 5–4) follow at the end of this chapter.

Prior to scanning your resume into its applicant-tracking system, the potential employer creates a list of keywords and phrases that best describe the position available, the job requirements, and the necessary skills. Your primary objective when creating a scannable resume is to make an educated guess and include as many keywords and phrases as possible that you think will match up with the list already entered into the computer. The resumes with the greatest number of matching words and phrases will be the ones the applicant-tracking software tags as representing qualified applicants; these are the resumes that the HR department or person in charge of hiring will most likely evaluate.

When creating a scannable resume (after you have determined what content to incorporate into your document) carefully read the ad to which you're responding and the job description the company has written for the position. Any keyword or phrase, industry buzzword, specific job title, years of experience, degrees or licenses required, skills, or personal traits, and so forth, mentioned in the ad or job description should definitely appear within your resume.

In essence, what you're creating is a keyword-based resume printed on paper that will be accurately scanned. Especially if you're applying for a job within a medium- to large-size company, developing this type of resume is critical, because more than 80% of employers are now using applicant-tracking software to assist in their hiring and recruiting.

An electronic resume can be imported into applicant-tracking software, and in most cases, should be created using a keyword style for it to have the most impact and generate the best results for you.

When creating this type of resume, some applicants choose to add a section near the top of their resume (below the heading and objective), called Keywords. This is simply a listing of keywords pertaining to your qualifications that the computer might be looking for.

As long as your resume focuses on information you know the employer is looking for, in a format the employer's computer system can understand, your chances of landing the job you apply for will be improved. The best way to ensure that you are submitting the right type of resume to a specific employer (i.e., a traditional printed resume versus a scannable resume) is to contact that company's HR department and inquire about how they evaluate incoming resumes. Also, ask if they have any specific submission guidelines.

Although computers have become an integral part of recruiting and job searching, it's still important to create a traditional printed resume that you can hand to someone at the start of a job interview, or mail if the company you're contacting doesn't use applicant-tracking software. Investing the time necessary to create both a readable resume and a scannable resume as your job-search process begins is definitely a worthwhile strategy. These two resumes should contain the same basic information (targeted to the job for which you're applying), but should be worded, and perhaps, laid out, differently on the page. Depending on the type of job you're pursuing, you also might consider creating an electronic or digital resume that can be sent via e-mail, added to online databases, or used when applying for a job from a website.

Exhibit 5–3. Sample Keywords Suitable for Scannable Resumes

Although there are literally thousands of industry and job-specific keywords and phrases you could incorporate into a scannable resume, here's just a small sampling:

- # Years' Experience
- Accounting
- Accounts Payable
- Accounts Receivable
- Adaptable
- Analyst
- Auditor
- BA
- Budget Analyst
- Conceptual Ability
- Contract Reviewer
- CPA
- Customer Oriented
- Dependable
- Detail Minded
- Direct Marketing Campaigns
- Director

- Enthusiastic
- Executive Assistant
- Financial Reports
- Flexible
- Follow-Through
- High Energy
- Human Relations Specialist
- Innovative
- Leadership
- Manager
- Market Analyst
- Market Researcher
- Marketing Business Plans
- MBA
- Microsoft Excel
- Microsoft Office 2000
- Microsoft Office User Specialist
- Microsoft Word
- Multi-Task Management
- Open Minded
- Ph.D.
- President
- Problem Solving
- Resourceful
- Results Oriented
- Sales Manager
- Self-Accountable
- Self-Managing
- Spreadsheet Development
- Strategic Planner
- Supervisor
- Supportive
- Takes Initiative
- Team Oriented
- Trade Show Management
- Trainer
- Travel and Meeting Planner
- Vendor Coordinator
- Vice President
- Willing to Travel

Exhibit 5–4. Sample Scannable Resume

Joel E. Wilner
896 Winter Ave #7J
Brooklyn, NY 11238
718-555-4321
j-w@blankslate.com

OBJECTIVE: To work in an environment in which I can use my strong writing skills and gain knowledge of the publishing world.

EDUCATION: **Bachelor of Arts in English**, Writing Emphasis, June 2005
University of Washington, Seattle, Washington
Dean's List
GPA of 3.7 on 4.0 scale

Relevant Courses:
- Travel Writing
- Fiction Writing
- Public Relations Writing
- Analytical Writing

EXPERIENCE: *Tutoring Coordinator and Teacher*, September 2003–June 2005
After-School Association, Seattle, Washington
- Oversaw after-school tutoring program for 25 elementary school children in a low-income community.
- Organized and led educationally enriching activities focused on basic reading, math, and problem solving.
- Supervised eight tutors.

Teacher, October 2004–June 2005
Whiteview School-Age Childcare, Seattle, Washington
- Supervised children in an integrative before- and after-school program.
- Planned and executed daily activities emphasizing multicultural awareness, life skills, computer proficiency, and fun.
- Developed negotiating and problem-solving skills.

SKILLS: - Leadership experience
- Team oriented
- Italian language
- Microsoft Office 2000 (Word, Excel, Outlook, PowerPoint)

ACTIVITIES: Studies Abroad, Siena, Italy, 2004 and Golden Key Honor Society 2002–2005

creating and submitting your resume package: from cover letters to thank-you notes

YOUR RESUME IS just one of the tools you will use to ultimately land a new job. This chapter deals with assembling the perfect resume package, which consists of:

- Your resume
- Your cover letter
- References
- A personalized business card
- Samples of your work (if applicable)
- Thank-you notes

> **The key to creating a professional resume package is *synergy* when it comes to appearance and content: All the parts of the package should work together to create a greater overall effect. You should use the same paper, fonts, and typestyles when creating these documents.**

Later in this chapter, methods of actually getting your resume into the right hands are explored. These methods include responding to an ad, networking, and taking advantage of career-related websites.

WRITING A COVER LETTER

One of the most common misconceptions among job seekers is that the resume is their primary marketing tool when looking for a job, and the cover letter is nothing more than an ancillary formality. In reality, your cover letter is as important as your resume when it comes to capturing the attention of a potential employer and selling yourself as a viable candidate for a job opening.

Because e-mail, faxes, and other written correspondence have become the primary methods of communication in today's business world, many employers rely on the cover letter to evaluate a candidate's ability to communicate in writing. Virtually all employers put great value on an applicant with strong written and oral communication skills. After all, a resume is typically a series of bulleted lists and short sentences, but a cover letter represents an actual *writing sample.*

Unless you first impress an employer with your cover letter, many HR professionals won't bother to read your resume. Thus, there's a chance your cover letter will be your only opportunity to convince a potential employer that you are a viable job candidate. Both the wording and the overall appearance of your cover letter should complement your resume.

Your cover letter should not duplicate too much information that's already in your resume. Use your one-page cover letter as a marketing tool designed to:

- Introduce yourself
- State the specific job for which you're applying
- Seize the reader's attention
- Pique the reader's interest
- Convey information about yourself that's not in your resume
- Briefly demonstrate your skills and accomplishments
- Convince the reader to read your resume
- Ask the reader for an action to be taken

Every cover letter should highlight things about you that are of direct interest to the recipient. Before sending a resume and cover letter to an employer, you must first develop an overall message and package to market yourself. This package should be synergistic.

As previously mentioned, the envelope, stationery, ink color, typestyle, and font should all match, and each piece in your resume package should work together to promote you—the applicant. Every aspect of your overall package can affect the decision to invite you in for an interview or not.

CREATING YOUR RESUME PACKAGE

A resume package consists of your resume, cover letter, envelope, and any additional documents you eventually supply to a potential employer, such as a list of references or a thank-you note, in hopes of landing an interview. This chapter emphasizes that using matching papers, envelopes, ink colors, typestyles, and fonts for each document in your resume package is essential for many reasons.

Your resume package will most likely arrive on a potential employer's desk along with many other pieces of mail, and possibly dozens of other resumes from people applying for the same position. Someone will sort that mail, and your resume package will, hopefully, reach its intended destination—the HR person or executive within a company who is expecting to receive it.

If you want your resume package to stand out, it needs to look professional, as if you've put considerable thought and attention into the appearance of the package. First impressions, in this case, are important. The first impression your resume package makes is based on its appearance.

....

Sending an unsolicited resume to an executive within a company is like sending a piece of junk mail. Only a small percentage of unsolicited resumes a top-level executive receives actually get read. Most executives will simply forward your resume to the company's HR department, though some may just toss your resume in the trash. Writing Personal or Confidential on a resume sent blindly to an executive is almost guaranteed to get it tossed without ever being opened.

....

YOUR RESUME PACKAGE'S APPEARANCE

Although the content of your resume, cover letter, and all other documents supplied to a potential employer is important, the initial objective of your package is to *capture the attention* of the reader by making your resume package look spectacular, yet highly professional. Of course, having some graphic design experience helps, but it's certainly not necessary as long as you follow basic design rules.

To accompany your resume, it's important to include a well-written cover letter that will introduce yourself to a potential employer and hopefully convince the reader to review your resume.

INTRODUCING YOURSELF WITH A COVER LETTER

Your cover letter is used to introduce yourself to a potential employer, state the job for which you're applying, explain some of the reasons why your resume is worth reading, and then request some sort of action to be taken by the reader.

Although the reader of your cover letter will, of course, look at the letter's content and meaning, the reader will also be evaluating your writing style, spelling, punctuation, and the format of your document. What you say in your cover letter is important, but you should also think carefully about *how* you want to say it, and make sure that your overall presentation is professional and *visually* appealing.

Typically, cover letters should be written in a business letter format and customized to the job for which you're applying. Also, these letters need to be personalized, using the name and title of the recipient.

Anytime you submit a resume to a potential employer, it should be accompanied by a cover letter. The main exception to this rule is if you attend a career or job fair and you distribute resumes to a handful of employers while attending the event. Otherwise, always use a cover letter when:

- Sending a resume in response to a help-wanted ad or job opening announcement
- Following up on a job lead given to you by an acquaintance
- Sending an unsolicited resume to a company

Before sending your resume package to anyone, make sure you know the full name and title of the person you are addressing. Using the correct spelling of the recipient's name along with the company's name is important. It's also critical to confirm the recipient's gender, so you can address the envelope and cover letter to Mr., Ms., Mrs., (insert last name). Accidentally spelling someone's name incorrectly is insulting to the recipient and totally unprofessional. The slightest spelling error could result in your resume package getting thrown out, even if you're a qualified candidate.

Once your resume package is complete and you've found job opportunities to pursue, the next step is to pinpoint specifically to whom your resume package should be addressed. The cover letter and the envelope for your resume package could be addressed to any of the following people within a company, based on various circumstances:

- A friend, former business associate, or network contact who currently works for (or is associated with) the company for which you want to work. If this person isn't responsible for the company's actually hiring, your cover letter should ask him or her to forward your resume package on your behalf to the appropriate person, along with their recommendation.
- A professional headhunter or job placement specialist.
- An executive or department head at the company for which you want to work, such as the vice president of marketing if you're hoping to land a job within the company's marketing department.
- Someone in the HR department at the company for which you want to work.

The Anatomy of a Cover Letter

You must obtain and include the following information for your cover letter to have the desired impact. So, before you actually sit down to write a cover letter, make sure you know:

- The recipient's full name
- The recipient's job title
- The company name
- Mailing address
- Phone number
- The exact position for which you're applying
- The recipient's fax number (optional)
- The recipient's e-mail address (optional)

Your resume should summarize your accomplishments, education, and skills, using plain English. Thus, your cover letter should be used to complement your resume by offering an introduction and explaining what exactly you can do for the company for which you want to work.

Just as your resume was only one 8½-by-11-inch page in length, your cover letter should also be kept to one page. The shorter the better, because most people don't have time to read long letters.

***

Within your cover letter, it's acceptable to use bulleted points to emphasize key facts, skills, or elements of your work history. Using bulleted lists eliminates the need for long paragraphs of text and can make your cover letters easier to read.

***

At the top of your letter, list your full name, address, and phone number. If you have personalized stationery to match your resume paper, use it. Your contact information should be followed by the recipient's address and the date (using a standard business letter format). Next comes the salutation, the opening paragraph, your marketing message, one or two support paragraphs, your formal request for an interview, and finally some type of closure. Because your cover letter is so important, let's look at each of these sections in more detail.

The Salutation
Your cover letters should start off with a salutation, such as:

- Dear (insert job title):
- Dear (insert recipient's first name),
- Dear Mr./Mrs./Ms./Dr. (insert recipient's last name):
- Dear Sir or Madam:

Do not use "To whom this may concern." This is the worst salutation you can use for a cover letter. It's impersonal and demonstrates that you didn't take the time necessary to determine to whom the letter should be sent.

TIPS FOR ADDRESSING YOUR COVER LETTERS

1. Because you're writing a personalized cover letter to a specific individual, the salutation should read, "Dear Mr./Mrs./Ms./Dr. (insert recipient's last name)." Avoid addressing someone by his or her first name unless they're a relative or close friend.

2. If you're responding to a help-wanted ad that only lists a contact person's first name, and no telephone number, then obviously you should address your cover letter to that person using his or her first name. Never use a generic salutation, such as "Dear Sir or Madam:" or "Dear (insert job title):" unless you have no other option. And, never address a letter to "Dear Sir," assuming your reader is a man. Many women managers will automatically toss cover letters addressed this way, simply because you have assumed that the person in charge of hiring is a man. You do not want your resume ignored because of such a simple mistake.

3. Unfortunately, some names, such as Pat, Chris, Kim, Jamie, or Sandy, can belong to either a male or female. Before sending your package, determine the gender of the recipient by calling the company and asking the receptionist; *don't* ask to speak to the person to whom you're writing (or even his or her assistant). Most companies are adamant about "no phone calls" from candidates responding to help-wanted ads, and you should respect that policy (even if it's *not* stated). If you cannot obtain the information regarding the person's gender, as a last resort, you could simply address your letter to "Dear Chris Smith," for example; Chris will appreciate your not having assumed his or her gender. Don't make assumptions.

4. If you're sure the recipient of your letter is a woman, but you don't know if she is married, the safest approach is to use "Dear Ms. (insert last name):" as your salutation. In today's business world, "Miss" is seldom used in a business letter and "Mrs." should only be used to address someone who is married and uses her married name.

The Opening Paragraph

The opening paragraph of your letter should be short and simple. Answer the questions "Who are you?" and "Why are you writing this letter?" Keep this part of your cover letter no longer than two or three sentences.

Examples of an opening paragraph might be:

I noticed your advertisement in the (insert date) edition of (insert newspaper/publication name), and strongly believe I have the skills and work experience necessary to fill the (insert job title) position that you have open. Enclosed please find my resume.

(Insert name) suggested I contact you regarding the opening for the (insert job title) position your company has available. Enclosed please find a copy of my resume for your consideration.

In response to our telephone conversation on (insert date), regarding the job opening (insert company name) has for a (insert job title), I am pleased to enclose my resume for your consideration.

In response to your company's ad, which appeared in the (insert date) issue of (insert newspaper/publication name), please consider me for the (insert job title) opening your company has available.

Our mutual colleague, (insert name of colleague), suggested I contact you regarding the (insert job title) job opening your company has available.

In the opening paragraph of your cover letter, mention specifically for what job opening you're applying, especially if you're responding to an ad.

Your Marketing Message

Following the opening paragraph, the next paragraph or two within the body of your cover letter should be used to quickly distinguish you from the competition and position you as the best applicant for the job.

One of your main goals for this section of the letter should be to address the employer's needs. You should have a basic understanding of what the employer's needs are from information such as the wording of the ad or job description. Give a few examples of how you can fill those needs.

One way to begin this paragraph is by posing a question (such as, "Don't you need…?"), however, a strong opening statement often works best. For this portion of your letter, using bulleted points can save space and allow you to convey more information to the reader quickly.

One approach you could take might read something like this:

For your consideration, enclosed is a copy of my resume, which as you will see, demonstrates some of the skills I possess and used regularly in my previous jobs:

- Accomplishment / Experience / Skill
- Accomplishment / Experience / Skill
- Accomplishment / Experience / Skill
- Accomplishment / Experience / Skill

If the ad to which you're responding states, for example, that "six years' experience as a sales account executive" within the employer's industry is a job requirement, address those needs directly. You could write:

As you'll see from my resume, I have (insert number) years' experience working for the (past employer's name) as a sales director. Some of my major clients have included: (insert company names). As a sales manager, I have developed an extensive client base, which in the past, has allowed me to be a top revenue producer.

In several short sentences, you can demonstrate how you meet the job opening's qualifications, and that you have related work experience. Answer the questions you know the potential employer has on his or her mind, for example:

- Are you knowledgeable about the industry and the company?
- Can you communicate well on paper?
- Do you possess the skills, education, and work experience necessary to meet the job's qualifications?
- Do you have what it takes to succeed at the company?
- What sets you apart from other applicants?

The Support Paragraph

What about the employer specifically piqued your interest? Answering this question should be the purpose of one of your cover letter's support paragraphs. Here's an opportunity to compliment the employer, demonstrate you've done some research about its organization and industry, and show that you have a strong knowledge regarding what the company is all about.

Be sure to emphasize your experience and accomplishments. Avoid personal topics such as your age, race, religion, health, physical/mental disabilities, hobbies, social security number, or references to your physical appearance.

....

When it comes to compensation (salary, benefits, etc.), avoid this topic in your cover letter. If your salary history is specifically requested, provide a range, not specific numbers.

....

As you create drafts for each cover letter, keep in mind that this too, like your resume, is a marketing tool. Include as many action words as possible. An extensive list of these words and phrases is provided in Appendix A.

A Request for Action

Typically, after responding to an ad or job opening announcement, the next step is to request a formal job interview.

This section of your cover letter should contain a request for the reader to take action and invite you for an interview. Remember, the person to whom you are writing is probably busy, so follow up with a telephone call and mention you will do so in your letter. Don't simply send out your resume package and then sit by the telephone waiting for a response.

This paragraph of your cover letter might be worded like one of the following:

> I plan on being in the (city, state) area on (insert date) and would greatly appreciate the opportunity to meet with you in person. I'll call you next week to schedule an interview.

> I'm looking forward to speaking with you in greater detail about this job opportunity. I will give you a call later this week to schedule a convenient time for an interview. In the meantime, please don't hesitate to give me a call at ###-###-####.

> Upon reviewing my resume, I hope you will find time in your busy schedule to meet with me in person regarding the (insert job title) openings at your company. I'll give you a call later this week to schedule a convenient time for a meeting.

> The opportunity to meet with you in person would be a privilege. To this end, I will contact you later in the week to schedule an appointment. In the meantime, please don't hesitate to give me a call at ###-###-####.

Closing

Your cover letter should conclude with a formal closing and your signature. Be sure to thank the reader for his or her interest, time, and consideration. A few ways to end the letter are:

Sincerely yours,
(Signature)
(Typed name)

Regards,
(Signature)
(Typed name)

Best regards,
(Signature)
(Typed name)

Yours truly,
(Signature)
(Typed name)

Respectfully,
(Signature)
(Typed name)

The wording of the final paragraph could be as follows:

Thank you, in advance, for reviewing my resume and considering me for the (job title) position you have available. I look forward to meeting with you in person for an interview soon.

Sincerely,
(Signature)
(Typed name)

Gathering the Facts Needed for a Cover Letter

Here's a short questionnaire to help you gather the information you will need when actually writing your cover letter. The answers you provide will help you write a well-organized letter that conveys the necessary key points.

Recipient (full name): _____

Recipient's gender: _____

Salutation for the recipient (Mr./Mrs./Ms./Dr.): _____

Recipient's exact job title: _____

Recipient's mailing address: _____

Recipient's phone number: _____

Recipient's fax number: _____

Recipient's e-mail address: _____

What position are you applying for? (Use the exact wording provided by the employer.) _____

_____

_____

How/where did you hear about the job opportunity? (If applicable, write down the date the ad was published and in what publication.)

_____

_____

Why are you qualified for the job? (List three skills/accomplish-ments/qualifications.) _____

_____

_____

_____

Why do you want to work for the company? (What appeals to you about the employer: its corporate culture, reputation, or its products/services?) _____

_____

_____

_____

What do you want to accomplish by sending this letter along with your resume? _____

_____

_____

What are the primary points (relating to your skills, work experience, and/or education) that you hope to convey within your cover letter?

_____

_____

_____

Develop a short (one- or two-sentence) synopsis stating who you are and what type of job you're qualified to fill. This statement should quickly summarize what's special about you as an applicant.

_____

_____

_____

Formatting Your Cover Letter on Paper

Traditional business correspondence can follow several basic formats, any of which are acceptable for a cover letter. With the possible exception of the thank-you note, all correspondence should be typed or created on a computer, as opposed to being handwritten. Exhibit 6–1 shows one example, and Exhibit 6–2 lists useful tips and guidelines for creating professional-looking cover letters.

Exhibit 6–1. Sample Cover Letter Layout

Your Name
Your Address
Your Phone Number
Your Fax Number (optional)
Your E-mail Address (optional)

Date

Recipient's Full Name
Recipient's Title
Company Name
Address
City, State, Zip Code

Dear (Mr./Mrs./Ms./Dr.) (Insert Recipient's Last Name):

Opening Paragraph

Support Paragraph #1

Support Paragraph #2

Request for Action Paragraph

Closing Paragraph

Sincerely,

(Your Signature)

(Your Full Name Typed)

The body of your cover letter can be left justified or fully justified, and it should be single spaced, printed using the same 12-point font as your resume, and use 1.25-inch left and right margins plus 1-inch top and bottom margins.

Exhibit 6–2. Tips for Creating a Professional-Looking Cover Letter

❏ Follow the format and style of a formal business letter.
❏ Use the same standard text font as the resume, such as Times Roman or New Century Schoolbook.
❏ Use an easy-to-read font size—between 10- and 12-point type—that matches your resume. A font size larger than 12 point will look unprofessional, and a font that's smaller than 10 point will be difficult to read.
❏ Make sure your cover letter is visually appealing and utilizes white space on the page.

❏ Make absolutely sure your cover letter is grammatically correct and contains no spelling or typing errors. Proofread each letter multiple times, and ask someone else to proofread it as well before sending it.

❏ Try to use standard 1.25-inch left and right margins and 1-inch top and bottom margins.

❏ Print your cover letter on a laser printer or high-quality ink jet printer. Using a standard typewriter will convey to the reader that you're not computer literate.

❏ Target and write each of your cover letters specifically for the job for which you're applying.

❏ Always personalize your cover letter, using the recipient's full name and title.

❏ In the salutation, write "Dear Mr./Mrs./Ms./Dr. (insert recipient's last name):"

❏ Keep your cover letters short (less than a full page).

❏ Write all of your sentences in less than 15 words and with a specific point. No paragraph should exceed three or four sentences. It can be appropriate to have one-sentence paragraphs within a cover letter.

❏ Use bulleted points whenever possible to keep your cover letter short yet still get your points across. Each bulleted item should be kept to one or two sentences, using as few words as possible in each sentence.

❏ If you're responding to an ad or job opening announcement, state specifically where you heard about the job opportunity. If you're acting upon a referral, mention the name of the person who referred you and his or her relationship to the reader.

❏ Avoid using clichés or overly used phrases. There is no need to re-introduce yourself by name in the body of the letter. Throughout the letter, try to be innovative and original with your wording, but not gimmicky.

❏ Within the first paragraph, specifically mention the position for which you're applying. Match the specific job title wording with the wording provided by the employer within the ad or job opening announcement.

❏ Don't lie or stretch the truth in your cover letter.

❏ Maintain a positive and upbeat tone throughout your letter.

❏ Make sure your letter flows and that the voice and tense used with the letter are consistent.

❏ Do not list your references within a cover letter; it's not necessary.

❏ Remove anything in your letter that's redundant.

❏ Make sure that your letter depicts you as someone who is career oriented and following a career path.

❏ Sign each letter using a black or blue ballpoint pen.

❏ Keep a copy of every letter you send out. Also, keep detailed notes regarding when each letter was sent, how it was sent, and what enclosure(s) were in the envelope.

❏ Never write "Personal" or "Confidential" on the envelope containing your resume package.

❏ Allow ample time for your resume package to arrive and be processed before making a follow-up phone call.

CREATE A PERSONALIZED BUSINESS CARD TO ACCOMPANY YOUR PACKAGE

To complement your resume and distinguish you from other applicants, have personal business cards printed with your contact information. These personal business cards should be included whenever you send a resume package and also with your thank-you notes.

For under $30, basic business cards can be printed that provide your contact information, including:

- Your full name
- Home phone number
- Cellular phone number
- Pager phone number
- Home and/or school address
- E-mail address

You can either have cards printed for you at a print shop, or you can buy special perforated stock either from an office-supply store and layout and print the cards on your PC. Again, it's best to use a laser printer.

It's important that the style of your personal business cards matches your resume in terms of paper color, font/typestyle, and ink color. The following is a sample layout for a personal business card that can be used as part of an overall resume package.

Daniel J. Lombardi
678 Broadway
New York, NY 10003

PHONE: 212-555-6543
FAX: 212-555-5432   E-MAIL: dlombardi@l&a.com

REFERENCES AND LETTERS OF RECOMMENDATION

Another valuable piece of your overall resume package, which will be submitted to an employer during a job interview or upon request after submitting your resume and cover letter, is your list of personal and professional references. Most companies will simply ask you to fill in this information on the company's standard job application, or the hiring manager or someone in the HR department may contact you (usually after an interview) and ask you to provide this over the phone or via e-mail. However, if you are asked to submit a list of references on paper, here are some guidelines.

From a visual standpoint, this document should be printed on the same type of paper as your resume and cover letter, and use the same font, typestyle, and ink color. In terms of content, your references should list the full name, address, and phone number of each person, plus a brief description of that person's relationship to you (i.e., friend, former coworker, former employer, college professor, etc.).

References should be separated into two categories—personal and professional. Personal references can include friends (but not relatives), past college professors (or high school teachers), and personal acquaintances who are well known or whose name will carry clout (such as the CEO of a well-known company, a politician, or a celebrity who knows you).

Professional references can include past coworkers, supervisors, or employers; leaders of charity organizations for whom you've done work; and so on. These people can vouch for your professionalism, work experience, and skills.

Instead of providing employers with a list of your references, you may be asked for letters of recommendation written on your behalf. Letters of recommendation should, of course, be written by the person recommending you and printed on his or her personal or company letterhead. These documents should *not* be printed on the same paper as your resume and cover letters.

REMEMBER TO SAY THANK YOU!

Immediately after every job interview, send the interviewer (or the person/people you met with) a personalized thank-you note to show your appreciation for taking the time to see you. Even if an employer wants to hire you, it's common for interviewers to hold out on making a job offer to see if an applicant sends a thank-you note in a timely manner.

Great Idea!

"Thank-you letters are a must! Get a business card from everyone you interview with so that you can get the names and titles correct on your thank-you letters, which should include a little tidbit of information from the interview so that they know you were paying attention. Don't copy the same letter over with the sentence order changed for different people within the same company. People don't usually compare thank-you letters, but you never know. In fact, a lot of folks just throw them out; but they do notice when they don't get one at all."

—Roz, Account Executive

No matter how busy and stressed you are about the job-search process, and even if you're 100% convinced that after participating in an interview that you're not getting hired, take a few minutes to write and send a personalized thank-you note within 24 hours after your interview. Sending a thank-you note is just one way you can set yourself apart from the competition, while demonstrating that you have strong follow-up skills and are a true professional.

A thank-you note can either be typed, using a formal business letter format, and then printed on the same paper you used for your resume and cover letter, or you could handwrite your personalized message on a note card. If you handwrite the note, use a black or blue pen, and write extremely neatly. You can also send an e-mail.

When writing a thank-you note, follow these general guidelines:

- Remind the interviewer who you are and when you met.
- Thank the interviewer for his or her time and consideration.

- Once again, state the exact position for which you're applying.
- Briefly mention something specific from your interview (to jog the interviewer's memory regarding you).
- In one sentence, describe why you're the best applicant for the job.
- State how much you want the job and ask to be hired.
- If you have personal business cards printed containing your name, home phone number, and address, feel free to insert a card in the envelope with your note. This will help the interviewer remember exactly who you are.

··

Interviewers aren't the only people who should receive thank-you notes. Anyone who provided you career guidance or assistance should also be shown gratitude. Thanking people for their support will encourage them to assist you again in the future.

··

Creating a resume package, as you've probably surmised, is a time-consuming task. Once this aspect of your job-search process is completed and you've selected how you want your overall resume package to look, the next step involves finding the best job openings and then actually applying for those jobs.

GETTING YOUR RESUME INTO THE RIGHT HANDS

Research shows that a huge percentage of job openings never actually get advertised in the newspaper's help-wanted section or on an online job site. As a result, it's up to you, as the job seeker, to find the best job opportunities and apply for them. In addition to relying on the employment ads, take full advantage of your networking skills. Contact friends, acquaintances, past employers, coworkers (past and present), college professors, professional associations, relatives, and anyone else who might know of available job opportunities for which you'd be suited.

From an employer's standpoint, they want to hire people who come highly recommended. Thus, you will always have a better advantage when you approach a potential employer through a personal introduction. Once you know what type of job you want to pursue, think about people you know who already work in that industry (or for the company for which you want to work) and make contact with them. Even if you don't have a direct connection to a company, chances are a friend of a friend might know someone who can make an introduction for you, so don't be afraid to tap your networking skills.

> Never underestimate the power of a good network. When you're looking for a job, or even after you've found one, keep in touch with former classmates, friends, business associates, people you met at seminars and workshops, and even your family! You just never know who might have some useful information, advice, a contact, or a hot tip that leads you to an opportunity. A thriving, up-to-date network is more powerful than the classified ads, the Internet, or the bulletin board at the community center.

The Internet is also a powerful job search tool. Hundreds of career-related websites are available, such as The Monster Board (www.monster.com), offering literally thousands of job listings. These listings are updated on an ongoing basis. Appendix C at the end of this book is a listing of career-related websites worth visiting.

Also on the Internet, newsgroups and mailing lists that cater to a specific interest or occupation can also be useful for finding job opportunities or networking with people currently working in your field. In addition, industry trade journals and newsletters along with industry-oriented trade shows provide opportunities to learn who's doing what in specific industries.

No matter how you make contact with a potential employer, you will have the greatest level of success if you receive a personal introduction or already know someone working for the company for which you want to work. If you do not know anyone at a prospective company, send a cover letter and your resume to a company's HR manager: After all, it is HR's job to find new, qualified candidates. You should find out the name of the HR manager to whom you plan to write; do not just send a letter with the salutation, "Dear HR Manager," because your letter and resume are more likely to be read if you address them to an actual person who is actually working for the company in which you are interested. You can usually find out the name of the HR manager by calling the company's receptionist or by visiting the company's website—most of which have a section on "jobs" or "contact us," with instructions on how to apply to that company. Sending an unsolicited letter to HR is perfectly acceptable when you are just beginning your career.

That said, however, it is not a good idea to send an unsolicited resume to a hiring manager, *unless you know that person or have a mutual contact*, or until you have had years of experience in an industry and would really be writing more as a professional colleague seeking a high-level position. The hiring manager's primary job is *not* to screen resumes—especially if he or she isn't looking to hire anyone—so if you send your resume to these people, at best, they will simply route your resume down to HR, and at worst, they may ignore or toss your resume altogether. Typical managers may receive 50–100 e-mails a day, numerous phone calls, and lots of other unsolicited mail—so if they get something from someone they do not know, they are not likely to pay attention to it, and many managers have confessed to simply deleting e-mail messages—without even reading them—if they don't recognize the sender's name. *Do not let your resume be ignored!* Instead, send it to the right person—the HR manager.

And again, it's always best to address your resume to a specific individual within the company. Once you know to whom you want to send your resume package, if you've spent the necessary time creating an impressive resume package and you're qualified for the job for which you're applying, your chances of being invited for an interview increase dramatically.

electronic resources
and resumes

AS IF YOU didn't have enough to deal with as you embark on the whole job-search process, in recent years the way people find job opportunities, research companies, communicate with potential employers, and apply for jobs has changed dramatically. The Internet has become an incredibly powerful job-search tool for virtually everyone with basic computer skills and access to a computer, the Internet, and e-mail.

If you're planning to work for a medium- or large-size company, taking advantage of the Internet is important. This chapter will explore some of the ways you can use the Internet, not only to find some of the best job opportunities available, but to research potential employers and industries and submit your resume online as well.

Yes, the Internet is an important job-search tool. However, your job-search process should be multifaceted. Take full advantage of what's available online, but don't forget about the more traditional resources. For example, when looking for job opportunities, visit the various career-related websites, such as The Monster Board (www.monster.com) and other websites listed in Appendix C, but don't neglect reading your local newspaper's classified ads, networking, visiting your school's career guidance office, and tapping the other resources available to you.

This chapter will help you use the Internet. You will discover:

- How and where to find job opportunities online
- How to research companies and industries online
- What's available from the various career-related websites
- How to create an electronic resume
- How to submit an electronic resume via e-mail
- If it's worthwhile for you to submit your resume to online databases

THE RIGHT TOOLS FOR THE RIGHT JOB

No matter how you plan on using the Internet as a job-search tool, to take advantage of everything it has to offer, you will first need access to a computer that has a web browser and your own e-mail account.

If you don't already own a computer that has Internet access, ask a friend if you can use one of theirs. You can also visit the computer center at your school, obtain access to the Internet at most public libraries, or visit an Internet café. For a lot less money than it would cost to purchase a computer, you can purchase WebTV or another set-top box that connects to your television set and telephone line to provide you with dial-up access.

Many people who are currently employed and who have Internet access at work tend to use their computers during business hours to search for new employment opportunities. This is a *bad* idea for several reasons. First, there are ethical issues involved with using company-owned equipment for personal purposes, especially when you're on the job and being paid to do work on behalf of your employer.

Secondly, most employers can easily and legally track what you're doing with your computer, so they will be able to determine what websites you visit as well as read your e-mail messages if they choose. Thus, if you are trying to keep your job-search efforts a secret from your current employer, using your computer at work is often a sure way to get caught.

Once you have the ability to browse websites, and send and receive e-mail, you will have one of the most powerful job-search tools available at your fingertips—24 hours a day, seven days a week.

In order to pursue job openings advertised on the Internet, instead of using your traditional printed resume, you will need to spend time creating an electronic resume. Although the formatting and wording used in an electronic resume is different from what you typically find in a traditional resume, an electronic resume contains the same basic information—a heading, objective, skill summary, employment history, educational background, and so forth. People creating an electronic resume often opt to also include a keyword section. Under a Keyword Summary heading, you could list 10–15 keywords for which you think the employer will be looking.

When your resume is in an electronic file, it can be e-mailed to an employer, posted on a website, added to an online database, and imported into applicant-tracking software used by potential employers. Although you won't have to deal with issues like choosing resume paper, picking the perfect font or ink color, or formatting your resume to look perfect on the printed page, there are other issues to contend with when creating an electronic resume. If you created your printed resume on a PC, you already have an electronic file with which to work. If you had someone prepare your printed resume and don't have access to or can't use the electronic file, you will have to create your electronic resume from scratch.

HOW AND WHERE TO FIND JOB OPPORTUNITIES ONLINE

Appendix C of this book lists career-related websites that cater to job seekers. This is just a small sampling of the many sites available to you. A career-related site caters to job seekers by offering a wide range of online services, typically offered free of charge.

One of the most popular career-related sites on the Web (designed for all types of job seekers, at all levels) is The Monster Board (www.monster.com). This site offers career-related articles and advice, plus at any given time, offers a database of hundreds of thousands of job openings available nationwide.

Instead of painstakingly reading the employment section of your newspaper, which is time-consuming and typically lists only jobs in your geographic area, free services like The Monster Board allow you to use keyword searches to find the job opportunities for which you're most suited. The best thing about performing these online searches is that it doesn't take hours—it takes seconds.

Services like The Monster Board allow you to search for job openings based on a wide range of criteria, such as employer, salary range, job title, geographic area, industry, skill(s) required, and so on. Another advantage is that these services are updated in real time, so new job opportunities are constantly being posted by employers. Thus, if you visit a website such as The Monster Board on a Monday morning and do a search for accounting jobs in New York City, for example, by Monday afternoon or Tuesday morning, new job opportunities will most likely be posted.

Many daily newspapers now post their entire help-wanted section online as well as offering it in printed form. A growing number of newspapers also offer career-related websites that cater to their geographic area. For example, Careerpath.com (www.careerpath.com) is sponsored by a large group of newspapers and covers all geographic areas.

The various career-related websites also allow you to apply for jobs online using an electronic resume. So, if you come across what looks like the perfect job opening, instead of mailing your resume, you can apply for that job online (immediately) by sending your resume via e-mail to that employer.

Yet another service many career-related websites offer is an online resume database. You can add your resume to a large database (with thousands of other job seekers). These databases are made available to employers. If an employer is looking to fill a bookkeeping position, for example, the director of HR for that company can access a resume database, such as the one offered on The Monster Board, and perform a search for qualified applicants. The employer, upon accessing your online resume, can then contact you directly.

As a job seeker, it's typically free to post your resume to an online database. The primary exception to this is if you want to add your resume to a specialized resume database that caters to a specific industry or field. In most cases, however, posting your resume to an online database takes just a few minutes and is free. Although this is definitely not a sure-fire way of getting hired, there is always a chance that an employer will come across your resume and contact you. Pursuing this type of job search activity can't hurt, but it should definitely not be your primary way of finding opportunities.

Because so many different resume databases exist to which you can post your resume, for the best results pinpoint a handful of the most popular databases, based on the type of work for which you're looking. Choose five or so of the extremely popular, general interest, career-related sites, such as Hot Jobs and Career Mosaic, and then find a few databases that cater specifically to your industry, area of expertise, or trade. For example, most professional associations have their own website, and many allow their members to post their resumes. If you work in advertising, for example, find a few industry-oriented sites that cater to the advertising industry and post your resume on those sites.

The best way to find industry-oriented sites is to use any Internet search engine such as Yahoo! or AltaVista. If you already know the name of an industry or professional association that caters to your field, use that name as the search phrase. Otherwise, use search phrases that best describe the position for which you're looking. A listing of popular search engines is also included within Appendix C.

Aside from finding job opportunities, adding your resume to an online database, and being able to access free career-related advice, many of the specialized career-related websites also enable job seekers to perform company/industry research online. They offer a range of other services and features designed to make the job-search process faster, easier, and less stressful.

In addition to the many specialized career-related websites and those sites hosted or sponsored by professional associations or organizations, it's also an excellent strategy to visit the website of the companies for which you are interested in working. Most company websites offer company and product or service information and have their own job opportunities or employment pages where you can discover exactly what positions a specific employer has available, determine whom you need to contact within that company, and discover how that employer prefers to receive resumes and cover letters from applicants (via e-mail, fax, postal mail, etc.).

Finding a specific company's website is as easy as using any Internet search engine. Type in the company's name as your search phrase. You can also use a bit of common sense, because many company websites tend to be obvious—www.companyname.com. If, when using your Internet browser, you simply insert the company name, more often than not, you come across the company website for which you're looking.

Surfing the Web is much like channel surfing on your television when you don't have a clue what's on or what program you're in the mood to watch. As you visit career-related websites, industry-oriented sites, or company-operated sites, don't be afraid to follow hyperlinks to see where they lead. If there's a company you're researching, find out who their primary competitors are, and visit their websites as well.

With practice, surfing the Internet and finding specific information will be a fast and easy process, and one that you may find entertaining as well. However, don't get sidetracked. If you're looking for career opportunities, for example, don't let yourself surf to sites that don't relate to what you're looking for. Banner ads, hyperlinks, and other forms of Internet advertising often make it extremely appealing to visit sites you had no intention of visiting. Stay focused!

> **If you're applying for jobs at a local retail store or small business, having an electronic resume is far less important, because to apply for one of these jobs, you will most likely visit the employer in person to submit a resume, complete a job application, and perhaps be interviewed on the spot.**

DOING RESEARCH ONLINE

Finding job opportunities online is just one way job seekers can use the Internet. Once you pinpoint an industry you might want to work in, or find one or more employers for which you'd like to work, it's important to learn as much as possible about the opportunities available to you. Thus, performing research becomes an integral part of the whole process of landing a new job.

Before the Internet, if you wanted to learn about an industry or a specific company, you'd have to visit a library and read past issues of newspapers, magazines, and newsletters, delve through financial reports, obtain and read annual reports, and find other sources of information. Once you gathered information, you still needed to read it, word for word, to learn as much as possible.

Thanks to the vast resources available on the Internet, there's no need to visit a library, contact companies to request annual reports or press kits, or manually search through back issues of newspapers, magazines, or newsletters. Much, if not all, of the information you could possibly need about employers, industries, and specific jobs is available online.

Finding information about companies that don't yet have websites may be difficult, but performing research on specific medium- to large-size companies is possible. If you're looking to work for a small company, consider gathering information about its industry. Knowing the key players and what challenges the industry is facing as a whole will help you when preparing for an interview with a smaller company.

In addition to visiting a company's website, exploring the various news-oriented sites, plus services like PR Newswire (www.prnewswire.com) and Businesswire (www.businesswire.com), or financial-oriented sites, such as Fidelity.com (www.fidelity.com) or TheStreet.com (www.thestreet.com), will help you gather both industry and specific company information. Finding information about publicly traded companies is much easier, because so much information is available at the various financial and business-oriented sites.

Appendix C offers a listing of news-oriented sites worth visiting when performing research. At any of these sites, you can perform keyword searches to find the specific information for which you're looking. Another source of company information is the career-related websites. Many of these sites contain background information about the employers that advertise job openings on their sites.

. . . .

Highbeam™ Research, Inc. (www.highbeam.com) makes it possible to conduct research via the Internet simply by posing a question, in plain English. Upon asking a question, this site will launch a comprehensive, simultaneous search through an archive of 35 million articles in newspapers, hundreds of national and international magazines, newswires, more than 3,000 publishers, including transcripts, and more.

Instead of sifting through local, regional, and national newspapers and magazines looking for articles about companies in which you're interested, Highbeam Research allows you to access thousands of media outlets and conduct complete searches in minutes.

. . . .

HOW TO CREATE AN ELECTRONIC RESUME

As mentioned, if you're going to be applying for jobs online or submitting your resume via e-mail, you will need to create an electronic resume in addition to a traditional printed resume. You can create and distribute an electronic resume in a variety of ways. Keep in mind, there are no standard guidelines to follow when creating an electronic resume, because employers use different computer systems and software. Thus, it's important to adhere to the individual requirements of each employer in terms of formatting, saving, and sending your resume electronically.

File Format

Many companies accept electronic resumes in Microsoft Word or WordPerfect file formats. When creating your electronic resume using one of these software packages, pay careful attention to what format the finished document needs to be saved in before sending it to an employer. The majority of employers prefer to receive resumes in ASCII or Rich Text Format. Once you save your resume in a file format other than the program's proprietary format, you will probably have to further edit it in order to fix lost formatting (such as indentation or italics).

Another method is to complete an online-based resume form while visiting an employer's website or a career-related site. In order to keep incoming resumes consistent in terms of formatting, many websites designed for recruiting insist that all electronic resumes be created using a predefined template, or provide a detailed form that requests all pertinent resume information. The website then formats the information automatically to meet the employer's requirements. This information is kept on the company's server and you won't have a file to submit via e-mail.

When completing an online-based resume form, fill in all fields with the appropriate information only. Be mindful of limitations for each field. For example, a field that allows for a job description to be entered may have space for a maximum of only 50 words, so the description you enter needs to provide all of the relevant information (using keywords) but also be written concisely. Because an electronic resume is as important as a traditional one, consider printing out the online form first and then spending time thinking about how you'll fill in each field or answer each question.

Don't try to add information that wasn't requested in a specific field in order to provide more information about yourself to an employer. For example, if you're only given space to enter one phone number, but you want to provide a home and cell phone number, don't use the fields for your address to enter the second phone number.

In most situations, if an employer accepts electronic resumes, chances are those resumes are imported directly into applicant-tracking software. Thus, it is important that the software used by the employer be able to extract the specific information it's programmed to find in the resume document you submit. If you don't provide the right information in the right fields, your resume may be ignored or not processed correctly.

The majority of online resume templates you will encounter on the various career-related websites and sites hosted by individual employers follow the same basic format as a traditional chronologi-cal resume. You will be prompted to enter each piece of information in separate fields, and you will most likely be limited in the number of fields you can fill in order to convey your information.

Some employers give applicants the option to compete an online resume form or send an electronic file via e-mail. Unless your work history and other information fits nicely into the format the online form follows, opt to send your own electronic file via e-mail. This will allow you to more easily customize the format you use so you can best highlight your skills and abilities.

For an electronic resume to do its job correctly, it needs to be loaded with keywords that will result in your resume being selected when processed by a potential employer using applicant-tracking software.

Great Idea!

"Before you send out your electronic resume, be sure to send it to a trustworthy friend first so that he can tell you if it looks all right. Often, over the Internet, a document's format changes and therefore becomes difficult to read. I've thrown away many resumes without even looking at them because I couldn't glance at one page and easily pick out the most vital candidate information. It would be a shame to miss out on a job opportunity because of something so simple to check, especially if you spent lots of time making your resume look neat, balanced, and professional."

—BRITTNEY, HUMAN RESOURCES ASSOCIATE

When e-mailing your electronic resume to an employer, as a general rule, the document should be saved in an ASCII, Rich Text, or as a plain text file and inserted into your e-mail message or attached to it. Almost every company will specify which format it prefers. You might be able to send attached files in the word processor's proprietary file format, which will preserve the formatting (line spacing, tabs, bullets, bold text, etc.). If a plain text or ASCII file is requested, you can easily copy and paste it into the body of the e-mail message. Your e-mail program might support some formatting, but if you don't know what program the recipient uses, it's best to assume that his or hers doesn't.

Due to the threat of computer viruses, many employers refuse to accept e-mail messages with file attachments. Thus, if you send your resume file attached to a standard e-mail message, the chances of that message getting deleted are high.

When e-mailing a resume, the message should begin with and contain the same information as a cover letter. You can then either attach the file to the message or paste the text within the message. Be sure to include your e-mail address as well as your regular mailing address and phone number(s) within all e-mail correspondence. Never assume an employer will receive your message and simply use the reply function to contact you.

No matter how you submit your electronic resume, be sure to proofread it carefully before hitting the send button. Just as with a traditional resume, spelling mistakes, grammatical errors, or providing false information won't be tolerated by employers.

When creating an electronic resume to be saved and submitted in an ASCII format, follow these formatting guidelines:

- Put in hard returns where you want a line of text to break. Otherwise, text will automatically wrap to the next line.
- Avoid using bullets or other symbols. Instead of a bullet, use an asterisk (*) or a dash (-). Instead of using the percentage sign (%) for example, spell out the word *percent*. (In your resume, write "15 percent," not "15%".)
- Use the spell check feature of the software used to create your electronic resume and then proofread the document carefully. Just as applicant-tracking software is designed to pick out keywords from your resume that showcase you as a qualified applicant, these same software packages can also instantly count the number of typos and spelling errors in your document and report that to an employer as well.
- Don't use multiple columns, tables, or charts within your document. Instead of tabs, indent text using spaces.
- Within the text, avoid abbreviations—spell out everything. For example, use the word *Director*, not "Dir." or *Vice President* as opposed to "VP." For degrees, however, it's acceptable to use abbreviations like MBA, BA, Ph.D., and so forth.

When sending a proprietary word processor format file, such as a Microsoft Word file, it's also important to keep the formatting, such as the font, simple and basic. If the reader doesn't have the same fonts, for example, the document will look different from your version.

....

Knowing how to properly create and submit an electronic resume demonstrates at least some level of computer skill. If you have a personal website you want potential employers to visit in hopes they will learn more about you, be sure the site doesn't contain personal information you don't want the employer to discover or that the employer will have no interest in. Posting your resume and support materials on a personal website can be worthwhile, especially if you're hoping to land a job in a computer-related or high-tech field. Make sure your personal site contains only information of interest to a potential employer, not pictures from your last vacation or photos of your cat, for example.

....

Content

Because formatting within an electronic resume is often minimal, what you say within your resume is what ultimately gets you hired. According to www.eresumes.com, "Keywords are the basis of the electronic search and retrieval process. They provide the context from which to search for a resume in a database, whether the database is a proprietary one that serves a specific purpose, or whether it is a web-based search engine that serves the general public. Keywords are a tool to browse quickly without having to access the complete text. Keywords are used to identify and retrieve resumes for the user.

"Employers and recruiters generally search resume databases using keywords: nouns and phrases that highlight technical and professional areas of expertise, industry-related jargon, projects, achievements, special task forces, and other distinctive features about a prospect's work history.

"The emphasis is not on trying to second-guess every possible keyword a recruiter may use to find your resume. Your focus is on selecting and organizing your resume's content in order to highlight those keywords for a variety of online situations. The idea is to identify all possible keywords that are appropriate to your skills and accomplishments that support the kinds of jobs you are looking for. But to do that, you must apply traditional resume-writing principles to the concept of extracting those keywords from your resume. Once you have written your resume, then you can identify your strategic keywords based on how you imagine people will search for your resume."

The keywords you incorporate into your resume should support or be relevant to your job objective. Some of the best places within your resume to incorporate keywords is when listing:

- Job titles
- Responsibilities
- Accomplishments
- Skills

Industry-related buzzwords, job-related technical jargon, licenses, and degrees are among the other opportunities you will have to come up with keywords to add to your electronic resume.

Keywords are the backbone of any good electronic resume. If you don't incorporate keywords, your resume won't be properly processed by the employer's computer system. Each job title, job description, skill, degree, license, or other piece of information you list within your resume should be descriptive, self-explanatory, and be among the keywords the potential employer's applicant-tracking software looks for as it evaluates

your resume. One resource that can help you select the best keywords to use within your electronic resume is the *Occupational Outlook Handbook* (published by the U.S. Department of Labor). This publication is available, free of charge, online (http://stats.bls.gov/oco), however, a printed edition can also be found at most public libraries.

What Is ASCII Anyway?

When dealing with electronic resumes, you often read or hear the term ASCII. This is an acronym for American Standard Code for Information Interchange. It refers to the way information within a text file is saved. Because ASCII is a widely accepted standard (and understood by word processors, text editors, e-mail programs, applicant-tracking programs, etc.), using it increases your chances that the electronic resume you create will be compatible with the computer systems and software in use by potential employers.

If you're using Microsoft Word to create your resume and then save it in ASCII format, use the "Save As" feature found under the File pull-down menu. When asked for the "Save As Type" (under the filename), choose "Text Only." If your document contains special formatting, or symbols such as bullets, you may be asked if you want the software to fix your document and edit it so it fits properly into the ASCII format. Choose "Yes" to ensure your document will be easily readable. Much of the formatting will be lost, so you should review and edit the text file yourself.

Rich Text Format

Rich Text Format is a standardized way to encode various text formatting properties, such as bold, italics, and underlined characters. It also maintains a document's formatting. This type of file is compatible with most word processors and text editors. Because it maintains much, if not all, of the formatting in the document (i.e., how the document is laid out on the page), it's a good alternative to saving a file in ASCII format, which does not maintain any formatting but simply saves the text.

HTML Formatted Resumes

In addition to sending your electronic resume via e-mail or adding it to an online database, you can also create an electronic resume in HTML format and post it as a personal webpage. HTML is a programming language used to create websites. Using many popular word processors, you can automatically create HTML documents (without doing any programming), so the documents you create are compatible with the Internet and can incorporate such features as hyperlinks. When you create a document, such as a resume, in HTML format, it's easy to post that document on a website.

One advantage of HTML over other file formats is the hyperlink. You can make your degree program, school, past employers, or other items links to webpages that contain more information, such as your academic department or current company's home pages.

If you choose to create your own personal website, you will have to post your webpages on a server, somewhere. One method is domain name hosting: You register a specific domain name (yourname.com or yourname.org) with a registrar such as Network Solutions (www.networksolutions.com) or Registrars.com (www. registrars.com), and that name actually points to an Internet service provider's Web server. Some Internet Service Providers (ISPs) will take care of registering as well as hosting your domain name. The charge for registering a domain name is $35 per year. The cost to host a website can vary greatly. If you already have Internet access through an ISP, you may receive website-hosting services for free. Otherwise, plan on spending between $9.95 and $29.95 per month.

Members of online services, such as America Online, can receive free website hosting for personal webpages. This is a cheaper alternative, but your URL will be somewhat long and not easily memorable. Some online services, such as Geocities, host webpages for free, but all the pages display banner ads for various companies.

Unless you're looking to work in the computer field, setting up a personal website just for your resume probably isn't necessary or practical. However, HTML files are easily e-mailed and preserve a lot of the formatting created in word processor files. Some employers may ask for submissions in this format. If HTML is an option, it's usually a good choice. Word processors such as Word will save a document in HTML format. Basic HTML tutorials are also available online.

Conclusion

As companies of all sizes turn to technology to assist in their recruiting, the need for job seekers to have an electronic resume is increasing, especially if you're apply for a job at a medium- to large-size company. Computer literacy is a skill that virtually all employers require. So whether you choose to apply for jobs using an electronic resume or you use the Internet as a job-search and research tool, it's becoming more and more important for job seekers to tap the power of the Internet when looking for job opportunities, applying for jobs, or doing research.

Just a few years ago, using a computer to assist in your job-search efforts would have given you an incredible edge over other applicants. These days, however, not using a computer (and the Internet) as part of your overall job-search efforts puts you at a major disadvantage.

Because career-related websites can be updated in real time, 24-hours-per-day, as companies have new job openings, they can be posted instantly, allowing job seekers to learn about and apply for openings immediately via e-mail or by visiting a specific website. Those who surf the Internet and continuously look for the newest ads posted online are more likely to land a job than those who sit home reading the newspaper and submitting their resume via U.S. mail.

resume software makes the whole resume-writing process easier

AFTER YOU HAVE decided what you want to say on your resume and determined the best way to say it, one of the most time-consuming aspects of creating your resume will be actually formatting and laying it out on the page, especially if you're using a word processor. To make your resume look professional, you will have to deal with issues like tabs, line spacing, margins, and font sizes. There are, however, several ways to make the formatting process much easier and less time-consuming.

Microsoft Word comes with a pre-defined resume template you can use to assist in the formatting of your resume. If you already use Microsoft Word, this chapter will walk you through the resume-formatting process using this powerful word processor.

Aside from general-purpose word processors, there are a handful of off-the-shelf software packages designed specifically for creating, formatting, and printing resumes. These packages are available wherever software is sold, and some can be purchased and downloaded off the Internet.

Priced between $19.95 and $39.95, some of the more powerful resume-creation software packages are designed to assist you in virtually every aspect of your job-search process. For example, some have built-in contact management applications (for keeping track of potential employers) and an appointment book application (to handle the scheduling of interviews). Some packages are compatible with the various career-related websites and will automatically find the best job opportunities for you and help you apply for those jobs online.

Several of the resume-creation software packages also have built-in tutorials designed to help you prepare for your interviews, do company research, create your resume, and write cover letters. Thus, in addition to using the Internet as a powerful job-search tool, your computer can help you create highly professional printed and electronic resumes.

Great Idea!

Before you decide to use any resume software, be sure to do a bit of research. You will be investing a significant amount of money into the development of your resume, so you will want to make sure that the software is all it's cracked up to be. Your resume is your most important marketing tool. Be a proactive force and don't leave your future up to chance!

—EMILIA, EXECUTIVE MANAGER

RESUME SOFTWARE

This chapter offers information about several of the popular Windows-based resume-creation software packages available that run on PC-based computers. If you plan on creating your own resume from scratch, investing in any of these packages will save you time, plus help you keep your entire job search well organized. If you are using a Macintosh computer, try Printshop Publishing Suite from Mindscape.

Web Resume Writer

PRICE: $19.95
PUBLISHER: eInternet Studios
WEBSITE: www.web-resume.org

This resume-creation software package is available for purchase online only. Web Resume Writer is compatible with Windows 95/98/NT/2000/XP and is designed to make producing printed or electronic resumes easier. When using this program, you will have total control over your resume's layout, appearance, and structure. The software is powerful, yet its point-and-click interface is designed for people who aren't too computer literate. To help ensure your resume has the most impact, a spell checker and the ability to ultimately export your resume file into Microsoft Office applications (including Word) is provided.

To enhance the software's usefulness, the built-in contact management application will help you maintain a detailed database of potential employers and the contact people at each company. From this contact management module, it's possible to instantly send e-mail with attached resume and cover letter files.

As you create your resume using this software, you will be prompted to enter information for one section at a time, beginning with the heading. You can then choose which sections to include on your resume and enter the appropriate information into each section. The software has nine popular resume sections, including: Biographical Data, Purpose Narratives, Educational History, Employment History, Honors/Awards, Organizations, Skill Areas, Publications, and References.

Once the resume content is entered, you can begin experimenting with the layout, appearance, and organization of your resume. The final product can be printed, saved, exported to a word processor, or saved in HTML format with embedded hyperlinks.

ResumeMaker® Professional 12.0

PRICE: $29.95
PUBLISHER: Individual Software
            800-822-3522
WEBSITE: www.individualsoftware.com

This Windows-based software offers a complete set of integrated applications designed specifically for job seekers. In addition to helping you create a powerful paper-based or electronic resume, ResumeMaker allows you to easily tap the power of the Web (if you have access from the same computer on which you will have the program).

The software is compatible with 90 of the Web's most popular career-related sites and is designed to help you find the best job opportunities based on your search criteria and then apply for those jobs online using an automated process. The software also features a contact manager, designed to help you keep track of each potential employer and the contacts at each company.

ResumeMaker walks you through the entire resume and cover letter creation process using step-by-step directions that involve entering text into pop-up dialog boxes that prompt you for specific information. As you enter this text, the software even recommends appropriate wording by allowing you to access a listing of action verbs and other powerful phrases. With the click of the mouse, you can switch between popular resume formats, plus obtain advice as to which format best suits your personal needs. The software's resume database allows you to see professionally created resumes suitable for a wide range of job seekers, whether you're a recent graduate with little or no work experience, or someone actively pursuing one of 1,000 different careers.

The Virtual Interview feature contains tutorials and expert advice designed to help job seekers prepare for their job interviews and then negotiate the best possible salary and compensation package when the time comes for these discussions.

ResumeMaker is available for download from the company's website or can be purchased from software retailers nationwide. While the software is particularly useful for someone new to the whole job-search process, it can save anyone considerable time when it comes to creating, printing, and distributing resumes and cover letters.

WinWay Resume Deluxe 11.0

PRICE: $39.95
PUBLISHER: WinWay Corporation
            800-4-WINWAY
WEBSITE: www.winway.com

This Windows-based software package also offers ease of use (even if you're not highly computer skilled) along with a wide range of features for job seekers. In addition to offering useful modules, WinWay Resume Deluxe 11.0 can be integrated with the Web, making it easier to pinpoint job opportunities and apply for them online.

The AutoWriter feature allows you to choose from over 100,000 job-specific phrases, keywords, and action verbs designed to add power and impact to your resume as you create it. There's also a large database of sample resumes and tutorials to use when creating a resume for virtually any job title in any industry.

Once an electronic version of your resume is created using this software, you can easily go online and have the software post your resume to dozens of popular resume databases. Simply input your state and job title. Specific resume-creation templates have been designed for people:

- Applying for entry-level positions
- Applying for middle management-level positions

- Applying for executive-level positions
- Changing careers
- Hoping to advance their career within the same industry
- With a negative employment history
- Who have a history of changing jobs often

Once your resume is complete, the Letter AutoWriter will walk you through the cover letter writing and creation process, allowing you to create documents that are synergistic in look and content with your resume.

By taking advantage of your computer's multimedia capabilities, sound, video, and graphics are used to offer tutorials and career-related advice. Upon creating your resume and cover letter, the software's contact management module can be used for keeping track of the potential employers you contact.

WinWay Resume Deluxe 11.0 features easy-to-use mail merge capabilities, so the information within your contact manager can be easily incorporated into your cover letter, and other parts of your resume package. Using the e-mail features, sending electronic versions of your resume is a snap, since the Contact Management module allows you to store e-mail addresses as well as fax numbers and mailing addresses.

No matter which format of printed resume you create using WinWay Resume Deluxe 11.0, it will be created in a style that makes it scannable by applicant-tracking software used by many medium- and large-size employers. The Fit To One Page feature ensures that your resume content automatically gets formatted to fit on a single printed page. To add a touch of your own creativity, the software allows you to take advantage of built-in themes, typestyles, fonts, graphics, bullets, and borders.

WinWay Resume Deluxe 11.0 can be purchased and downloaded directly from the company's website or is available nationwide from software retailers.

• • •

Just because a resume-creation software package is designed to work in conjunction with one or more of the popular career-related websites, as a job seeker, you must continue to do your own research, networking, and legwork to pinpoint the best job openings available. Tapping the Web for job listings and employment ads should be just one of your methods for finding job opportunities. Remember, a huge percentage of job openings are never advertised.

True Careers® and ResumeEdge

PRICE: $39.95
PUBLISHER: True Careers
WEBSITE: www.careercity.com

This website offers a variety of resume-writing services. The most basic (and least expensive!) helps you create an ASCII or electronic resume that you can post to job boards or e-mail to employers that do not accept attachments. This pared-down resume style includes no fonts, graphics, or special characters; instead, it emphasizes content and is scanner friendly. In addition, as part of this service, the company combines the content of your new electronic resume with its professional Web layouts to create a compelling Internet-based resume located at the company's Web address. The company will return to you an electronic, ASCII, or Web resume within 48 hours of your providing your resume information.

The site offers a step-by-step resume builder that requires you to provide your name, e-mail address, and city and state before setting up the account. The wizard then requires you to enter your employment history and skills. The wizard is simple to use, and the resultant resume is simple yet professional looking.

Other features of the website include job searches and alerts, career articles (providing useful information on interview tips, salary negotiation, career advice, etc), sample resumes and cover letters, and links to an expert resume-writing service (ResumeEdge.com).

ResumeEdge.com has certified resume writers and offers a personal telephone interview, a free Web resume, and a fast turnaround of 72 hours. The services offered vary from editing resumes $119.95 (with cover letter $179.95) to resume writing $139.95 (with cover letter $199.95).

The site offers a step-by-step resume builder that requires you to provide your name, e-mail address, and city and state before setting up the account. The wizard then requires you to enter your employment history, education history, and skills. The wizard is simple to use, and the resultant resume is simple yet professional looking.

The Right Resume

PRICE: $29.95
PUBLISHER: Whirlwind Technologies
E-MAIL: jnixon@wwtech.com

Using this Windows-based software, you can create your choice of a chronological, functional, or targeted resume, plus store information for up to ten employers. The Right Resume uses a basic, yet functional word processor for creating cover letters, customizing your resume, and executing the mail merge feature for group mailings. Users can also generate different resumes easily and quickly from one data source without having to retype. Modifying or customizing a resume is a quick and easy task with this software.

Additional features include a 50,000+ word spell checker, a contact management database for tracking potential employers, a calendar for scheduling interview appointments, a mail merge feature for generating multiple personalized letters from one main document, and a power words list that can be accessed to add meaning and impact when creating your documents.

You can download an evaluation version of the software (with some of the print features deactivated) from the company's website for free. If you like the software, you can register it for $29.95 and print out your resume and cover letter documents.

Great Idea!

As you formulate your resume, be sure to show the results you achieved at your last job—"during this time profits reached an all-time high"—that kind of thing. Your potential employer will be impressed by the fact that you have something to show for all your hard work. An economy of words is crucial as well. Use power words and phrases to succinctly highlight your accomplishments.

—JULIAN, DIRECTOR OF STRATEGIC PLANNING

CREATING A RESUME USING MICROSOFT WORD

The Resume Wizard, along with the pre-defined resume templates built into Microsoft Word, are designed to make it easier for users to write and format their resumes using this popular word processing software. A Wizard is a program within Word that simplifies a complex task by asking you questions and formatting a document based on your answers. The Wizard dialogue window has four buttons at the bottom that you use to move between steps or to exit the Wizard: Cancel, Back, Next, and Finish. Unless you cancel or finish, you can go back at any point to a prior step.

If using Word 97 or Word 2000, start the Resume Wizard by selecting "New" under the File pull-down menu. This brings up a window with multiple tabs. Select the "Other Documents" tab. Within that interface, icons for several different templates and Wizards will appear. Scroll down and then double-click on the Resume Wizard icon.

The regular Word screen will appear, with a new window, called Resume Wizard, in the center of the screen. This Wizard allows you to create a resume template that's custom tailored to your personal needs. To continue, click the Next button at the bottom right of this window.

The Resume Wizard window will ask you to select a resume style. Your three main options will be:

- Professional
- Contemporary
- Elegant

You will see thumbnail previews of what each resume format looks like on the screen. Using the mouse, click the resume format of your choice and then click the Next button at the bottom to move on to the next step.

You will next be asked, "Which type of resume would you like to create?" Your options will include:

- Entry-Level Resume
- Chronological Resume
- Functional Resume
- Professional Resume

Click on your choice and again click the Next button to move on. You will next be prompted to enter your name, address, and the other information for the heading section of your resume. Within this window, enter the following information in the corresponding fields:

- Your Name
- Mailing Address
- Phone Number
- Fax Number
- E-mail Address

Once this information is entered in the provided areas, proceed to the next step. The Wizard will present a list of sections and will ask which ones you want to include on your resume. You can change the actual name for each section later. The following prompt will appear within the Resume Wizard window: *The resume style you've chosen usually includes these headings. Select check boxes for the headings you want.* The choices of sections vary based on the resume format you chose. If you chose the entry-level resume, you can select from:

- Objective
- Education
- Awards received
- Interests and activities
- Languages
- Work experience
- Volunteer experience
- Hobbies
- References

The list will differ if you told the Wizard to create a chronological, functional, or professional resume. Place a check by clicking on the box next to the resume sections you wish to include. When you're done, click the Next button at the bottom of the Resume Wizard window to move to the next step.

The Resume Wizard will next prompt you saying, *These headings are sometimes included in this type of resume. Select check boxes for headings you want.* Once again, use the mouse to select the additional resume sections you'd like to include within your resume. If you're creating an entry-level resume, your options might include:

- Extracurricular activities
- Summer jobs
- Summary of qualifications
- Community activities
- Professional memberships
- Accreditations and licenses

- Patents and publications
- Civil service grades
- Security clearance

The list will differ for chronological, functional, and professional resumes.

If you choose not to include any of these sections, simply don't add check marks next to any of the options. When you're ready to continue, click the Next button at the bottom of the Resume Wizard window.

Next you can add any customized resume sections that weren't already included within the template and re-order or remove headings. Near the top of the Resume Wizard window, you will be asked: *Are there any additional headings you would like to add to your resume?* There is a text field right below this prompt where you can type in any additional headings. Click the Add button after entering each one.

You will next see a list of the resume sections you've already selected to include within your resume. You can change the order of this list from this screen by selecting any of the headings (click on the heading in the list and it will become highlighted) and clicking on the Move Up or Move Down buttons. You will have to use the up and down scroll-bar buttons to read the list. You can also remove any of the sections by clicking on the Remove button once the heading to be deleted is highlighted. When all of your resume sections are present in the list and in the desired order, click the Next button to proceed.

The Wizard now has enough information to format the resume and a customized resume template is now created. To complete this process, click on the Finish icon located at the bottom of the Resume Wizard window.

You will now be returned to the main Microsoft Word screen. The open document will be your customized resume template. You can now fill it in with content. Using the mouse or directional arrows, go through each line of the resume and type your personalized information within each section. The computer will automatically format what you type so that it fits within the resume style.

Also appearing on the Word screen will be the Microsoft Office Assistant, an animated character, which probably looks like a paper clip with eyes (this is a default option that you can change). Using this assistant, you will be given the following options:

- Add a cover letter (which opens another template)
- Change the visual style of the resume (you can switch between Professional, Contemporary, or Elegant)
- Shrink to fit (adjusts the type size, spacing, and margins so that your resume information fits nicely on an 8½-by-11-inch page)
- Send resume to someone (you can automatically e-mail or fax your resume)
- Get help on something else

If you don't want to take advantage of these options from the Office Assistant, click on the Cancel button in the dialogue bubble that appears near the paper-clip character.

Once you've entered all of the information within the resume template, you can save the document just as you would any other Word document. Move the cursor to the File pull-down menu and click on the Save option. You can then enter a filename and choose the file format in which you want your resume saved. The default option is in Word format, but you can also save the file in Text Rich Format, Text Only Format (ASCII), formats compatible with older versions of Word, or as a WordPerfect file. Printing the document is as easy as selecting the Print option from the File pull-down menu.

Using Word's Resume Wizard, you can also print matching envelopes and cover letters to accompany your resume. Once your resume is complete, you can take the document created in Word and edit or further customize it by changing the font, type size, or other visual details. You can download additional Word templates by visiting the Microsoft website (www.microsoft.com). These templates give you greater flexibility when creating your resume and cover letters.

If you decide to create a resume that contains multiple pages, access the View pull-down menu and select the Header and Footer options. This will allow you to customize the information to appear in the top or bottom margins on subsequent resume pages.

ACT! 2000

PRICE: $199.95
PUBLISHER: Symantec Corporation
WEBSITE: www.symantec.com

If using Microsoft Word (or another popular word processor) to create your resume, ACT! 2000, one of the best contact management and scheduling software packages on the market, can also be used to make your whole job search easier.

ACT! 2000 integrates with word processors, such as Microsoft Word. As a job seeker, you can create your resume and cover letters in Word (using the Resume Wizard or creating the documents from scratch). Next, create a database using ACT! containing all of your potential employers (including their names, addresses, phone numbers, fax numbers, e-mail addresses, notes, etc.). Using ACT! 2000's mail merge, you can then send out mass mailings via U.S. mail, fax, or e-mail with ease.

Because notes can be added to each person or company within your ACT! database, you can keep track of exactly when your resume was sent, to whom it was sent, what other enclosures you included, and the specific job for which you applied. You can also add all of your company-related research to your ACT! records.

Later, when someone from a company contacts you about an interview, you will have your notes available at your fingertips. You can also schedule your interview using ACT! and add notes about what was discussed on the phone into the contact person's ACT! database record.

Once you land a job, ACT! 2000 is an incredible tool that can be used in your professional life to help you keep track of all your contacts, appointments, written correspondences, and e-mails. People working in a wide range of jobs, in virtually all industries, have found ACT! to be an incredible time management and organizational tool. A free trial version of the software can be obtained from Symantec's website.

WHO NEEDS RESUME-CREATION SOFTWARE?

If creating your own resume from scratch, whether it'll be printed, e-mailed, or faxed, using resume-creation software helps you create and format your resume faster. Any of these software packages will also allow you to quickly make changes to your resume so that it can be customized for each job for which you ultimately apply.

Using resume-creation software is designed to save you time formatting your resume and making it look nice, but none of these packages can write your resume for you or choose the best format and wording to meet your personal needs. Thus, there's no short cut for spending the necessary time to determine what information about yourself belongs on your resume and then determining the best way to convey that information so it has the greatest impact on potential employers. The questionnaire offered within Chapter 2 continues to be important, as are the exercises in Chapter 4 that help you create the content of your resume.

• • •

Just because the software allows you to create a visually impressive resume, the content of your resume is still *your* responsibility to create. It's ultimately the content of your resume that
needs to pique the interest of the reader, so what you say has
to have an impact. It also needs to be catered to what you
believe the employer is looking for in terms of qualifications,
skills, and experience.

In the following interview, Erez Carmel, vice president of marketing for WinWay Corporation, explains some of the reasons why
job seekers should purchase and use resume-writing software when
embarking on a job search.

Why should someone use resume-creation software?

EREZ CARMEL: Why do actors, athletes, and other high-profile
celebrities use an agent to represent them? Because an agent knows
how to market their talent, and marketing talent is a unique skill all
by itself. Yes, anybody can write a resume, but will it make them
look as good as it should? This is where WinWay Resume comes in.
Our software provides the content and the format for the resume,
and makes sure you do not miss anything that could make you look
good to an employer.

For example, you may write in your resume, *"I managed a store,
hired and fired employees, and explained the products to the customers."* If
you use the AutoWriter feature of WinWay Resume, your resume is
more likely to read *"I managed the most profitable store in the chain, had
the lowest employee turnover rate, and made sure that each and every customer that came to the store was fully satisfied before they left."* Wouldn't
you think that this will make an employer more likely to invite you
for an interview?

What does this type of software help someone do that a standard word processor can't?

WinWay Resume gives you the content and the format for your resume. A word processor gives you a blank sheet and you have to add both content and format. Yes, you can use a word processor to write your resume, but will it have the right content? Will it put your best foot forward? WinWay Resume makes sure you will look your best and have the best chance of getting the job.

What are some of the key features of WinWay that set it apart from other resume-creation software products?

WinWay Resume contains more than 12,000 sample resumes, catering to thousands of professions, ready to work for the job seeker. Whether you are an architect, a nurse, an accountant, or a zoologist, your resume is already in there. We wrote it! To access these resumes, select File, Open Sample, then choose More Samples, and enter a few keywords describing your profession. You will get a long list of resume samples in the appropriate professions.

What type of job seeker will benefit most from using your software?

Any job seeker will benefit from it because it will make their job search quicker and more efficient. I think any job seeker would love to get a higher-paying, more satisfying job faster.

How long does it take for someone to create a powerful resume using your software?

It depends on the number of past jobs that you will want to describe. A typical one-page resume can be created in about ten minutes. However, I would recommend users spend a lot more time using our AutoWriter feature to make each and every phrase as powerful as it can be.

How much computer knowledge is needed to use your software?

The software only requires basic computer skills. If you can use a mouse and a keyboard, you can use WinWay Resume.

What are some of the common resume-creation mistakes that some-one can avoid by using your software?

By far, the most common mistake is describing *job duties* rather than *accomplishments*. If an employer is looking for an accountant, he or she takes it for granted that you can add and subtract numbers. What will make you get the job is showing the *unique value* that you added to the organization [past employers] through your *innovation* and *creativity*.

The AutoWriter feature of WinWay Resume offers you "fill-in-the-blank" phrases that are structured to highlight accomplishments rather than duties alone. We have also seen resumes that contain information that does not really belong in a resume, such as age, marital status, and other information that employers are not allowed to consider when making a hiring decision. Also, we have seen many resumes with spelling errors and inconsistent format. WinWay Resume helps avoid all these problems and creates a resume that will give you a better chance of getting the job.

What tips can you offer to someone creating a resume using your software?

WinWay Resume contains an incredible amount of multimedia content to help job seekers prepare for their job searches. There are numerous videos on topics from choosing the right paper and font to how to dress for an interview. There is also interview simulation in full-motion video with answers to more than 200 most commonly asked questions. We recommend that if job seekers can afford the time, they should watch all the videos first so they get first-hand understanding of what employers are looking for and how to best address the employer's needs in their resumes and cover letters. They should also use the online job search features of WinWay Resume to look at job ads in their areas and see what employers are looking for. At that point, they will be prepared to write their own resume, and make that person's resume really stand out from the rest.

Even if someone uses your software, what work/research will he or she still need to do in order to create a powerful resume?

WinWay Resume has everything you need to create the resume and get the job. However, we advise that before you send the resume, you talk to your references and prepare them for the possibility that somebody will call and ask about you. You should make sure they remember all the nice things you have done, and are willing and able to answer questions about you.

Anyone going through the whole job-search process, from finding job opportunities, submitting resumes, interviewing, and everything else that landing a new job entails, will definitely find using resume-creation software (or Microsoft Word combined with ACT! 2000) to be extremely helpful.

Great Idea!

You'll want to adjust your deportment to the particular situation, but it usually doesn't hurt to smile a lot and generally act like a person that other people want to work with. If you got an interview, they probably feel good about your technical abilities; now you have to sell the "sizzle" as much as the steak. Be ready to get into the nitty-gritty also, and if you haven't had much inter-view experience, get a friend to dry-run it with you. Get a book of interviewing questions and do some practicing.

—HANK, SYSTEMS INTEGRATOR

hiring a professional resume writer

WHEN IT COMES to writing a powerful resume, it's necessary to take full advantage of whatever written communication skills you have, whether they're based on natural ability or the result of years of studying and hard work. Unfortunately, not everyone has mastered the ability to communicate well in writing. If you fall into this category, one of the first things you should do in order to enhance your overall skill set and make yourself more marketable in the corporate world is find ways to improve your business-writing abilities. This can be done by taking classes, participating in home-study courses, or reading books and writing and rewriting. In the immediate future, however, you might consider hiring a professional resume writer to assist in creating the best possible resume on your behalf.

Although you may be totally qualified for the job for which you're about to apply, unless you have the ability to communicate your knowledge, skills, and experience in writing, your chances of being overlooked by a potential employer are high.

A professional resume writer can take all of the information you provide about your career objective, skills, educational background, and previous work experience, and then create your resume using the format the writer believes will best showcase and market your abilities.

Even if you know your writing skills need work, you can still take advantage of resume-creation software (discussed previously in Chapter 8) to create your own resume, because the software is designed to walk you through the entire resume-creation process and assist you in choosing the best possible wording. If you're willing to make a slightly higher financial investment in your job-search efforts, hiring a professional resume writer can often help you more swiftly land a higher-paying job, because your resume will work harder and become an extremely useful marketing tool.

Professional resume writers come from a wide range of backgrounds. Many are former educators, professional writers or editors, career counselors, headhunters, or human resource professionals. These people typically know exactly how the whole job-search process works and therefore can create resumes for their clients that are specifically designed to get attention.

Depending on the individual you hire to create your resume and the services he or she offers, the fee structure will vary greatly. For most job seekers, having your resume professionally written should cost between $50 and $300, depending on who you hire and how much work is required to create your resume.

If you have already tried to create your own resume, but you're simply not pleased with the final results, many professional resume writers offer less expensive critiquing services. So, instead of writing your resume from scratch, he or she will simply take what you created and improve it, or make suggestions on what you can do to enhance it.

The best way to find a talented professional resume writer is through a personal referral or word of mouth. Ask friends and family who have recently found new jobs if they used a professional resume writer. Also, many colleges and universities offer resume-writing services or workshops for free (or for a small fee), and you can likely obtain a list of professional resume writers from your school's career services office.

The Internet is also an excellent resource for finding professional resume writers, because many of these services operate primarily over the Internet and communicate with clients via e-mail and telephone. Using any Internet search engine or information portal (such as Yahoo!, Excite!, or AltaVista, for example), enter a search phrase such as "resume preparation," "resume creation," "resume writing," or "resume tips" to find a listing of the websites of professional resume writers available for hire.

Another excellent resource for finding a resume writer is the Professional Association of Resume Writers and Career Coaches (www.parw.com). This is an organization that makes its membership list available to potential clients.

Even if someone is a member of the Professional Association of Resume Writers and Career Coaches (or another professional organization, such as the National Resume Writers' Association), before hiring a professional resume writer, there are a variety of questions you should ask, listed in Exhibit 9–1.

Exhibit 9–1. Questions to Ask a Professional Resume Writer

❑ What services are offered?
❑ What do these services cost? Do you charge per hour, or is there a flat fee?
❑ What are your credentials?
❑ Can you create the type of resume I need (a traditional printed resume, a keyword resume, or an electronic resume)?

❏ Can you create a resume in HTML format?

❏ Will I receive my finished resume in printed or electronic form (on disk)?

❏ Is there an extra charge to update or customize my resume for a specific employer? If so, how much?

❏ How long have you been in business?

❏ How many resumes have you created for clients?

❏ In the past, have you created resumes for someone in my field?

❏ Will you provide me with testimonials from past clients or samples of your work?

❏ What process do you use for gathering the information to be included for my resume (an in-person interview, telephone interview, written questionnaire, e-mail questionnaire, etc.)?

❏ Once I provide you with my personal information, what process do you use for actually creating my resume? Will it be created from scratch, or do you simply plug the information into resume-creation software?

❏ What's the turnaround time once I hire you?

Although it may seem like there are a lot of questions, keep in mind that by working with a professional resume writer, you are hiring someone to create a document that represents you to potential employers. This document will be *the first impression you make* when contacting companies. The quality of the writer's work could easily determine whether or not an employer will consider you for a position and how highly a company will value you.

Because you will be providing the professional resume writer with personal information, it's important that you feel comfortable working with the person you ultimately hire. Once you choose someone to create your resume, it's vital that you provide him or her with as much truthful information as possible about yourself, your skills, educational background, and employment history. No matter how good a resume writer is, he or she is not a mind reader. The quality of raw information you provide the writer will greatly determine the degree of impact your resume will have.

Great Idea!

"Resume professionals know the business. Most have been on both sides of the process; they have been both hirers and hirees. A professional knows how to present a candidate's skills in the best possible light using key-words, action verbs, and power phrases."

—Mike, Sales Planner

If you're already somewhat successful in your field and looking for a better job that offers greater career growth potential and the ability for you to earn a higher salary, investing in the services of a professional resume writer is just one additional thing you can do during your job-search process to ensure you will achieve your objectives.

On the other hand, if you are seeking an entry-level position, you probably have limited work experience and are still developing your skills. Thus, you will probably be fine writing your own resume or taking advantage of resume-creation software.

TALK WITH A RESUME PREPARER

Regina Pontow is a professional resume writer who has created more than 2,500 resumes for clients around the country. Through her Proven Resumes website (www.provenresumes.com), Pontow offers online resume-writing workshops, free tips for writing resumes, and also promotes her personalized resume-writing services.

Pontow has been writing resumes professionally for more than a decade. Prior to starting her own Internet-based resume-writing business, she owned a personnel agency. Before that, she worked for the University of Washington in Bothell, Washington as a job placement specialist. She's also the author of several career-related books and continues to hold resume-writing seminars at colleges and universities.

The Provenresumes.com website was launched in 1997 and currently receives more than 1 million visitors per year. The site offers more than 100 pages worth of free information to job seekers. You can reach Pontow's resume-writing service via the Web. The prices for her resume-writing and resume-critiquing services start at $150, and her typical clients' salaries range froom $20,000 to $250,000. The advice Pontow offers within this interview, however, will be beneficial to all job seekers.

Why should someone hire a professional resume writer?

The biggest problem with job seekers is that they don't know how to pull out and describe the content in their resumes. There is so much information job seekers take for granted about themselves. If a potential employer were to discover some of that information, it would increase the applicant's chances of landing the job. For example, people don't know how to explain their work-related responsibilities, especially if they have generic-sounding job titles. One recent client I had worked for The Walt Disney Company and held the title "Area Manager." This title said nothing about what he actually did and the title itself didn't sound too impressive. Once I started asking questions, however, I learned my client was responsible for training and supervising over 450 employees who worked within one of the Disney theme parks. It turned out my client had extremely marketable management skills that he needed to showcase in his resume.

Many industries, like retail, offer job titles that aren't descriptive. Thus, as a resume writer working for my clients, I ask many questions in order to pinpoint what's special about each of them as an applicant and try hard to determine the most important pieces of information to highlight in each resume.

I believe the biggest reason someone should hire a professional resume writer is because we know how to extract information from our clients and use that information to the client's utmost advantage within the resume. A resume writer also knows exactly how to select a resume format that's most suited to the job seeker. We understand how to take advantage of each resume format, as necessary, when communicating information about our clients.

Are there certain types of job seekers than can benefit most from hiring a professional resume writer?

Just about anyone can benefit from the resume-writing services someone like me offers, especially people who have a hard time conveying their thoughts in writing. One thing people should realize, however, is that while there are thousands upon thousands of people advertising resume-writing services, there aren't too many really talented resume writers out there.

When interviewing a potential resume writer you might hire, make sure they've already written resumes for other people working in your field or who applied for the same type of position as you. Some people specialize in helping clients in specific income areas of industries. Be sure to ask about the resume writer's success stories and determine specifically how they interact with clients. I believe the best way to extract information from a client is by asking dozens upon dozens of questions. Some resume writers, however, will simply take the notes provided by their client and create a resume based only on that information.

What are some of the services a professional resume writer provides?

Virtually all resume writers also write cover letters for their clients, sometimes for an additional fee. Once I work with a client, however, they typically develop a good enough understanding of their own qualifications and strengths so they can write their own cover letters and customize them for each employer. The majority of job seekers, however, want their cover letters written for them as well.

For people who will be job searching online, they will want to have an electronic resume created that takes full advantage of keywords.

Creating an electronic resume requires different skills than creating printed resumes, so the job seeker should make sure these are skills the person they hire possesses. Web-based resumes are in essence personal webpages created in the style of a resume. This too is a service that some professional resume writers offer.

What should someone expect to happen once they hire you?

I begin by asking the client to send me whatever resume they currently have. I then ask about the salary range they're looking for, and specifically what type of job they're looking to fill. As part of this process, I ask the client to send me two or three help-wanted ads that represent the type of job they'd want and believe they're qualified to fill. I then read all of that information and create a long list of questions for the client.

Once I receive responses to those questions, I begin to actually write the resume. The writing process alone takes several hours to complete. In addition to the responses to my questions, I expect the client to provide a complete employment history.

What are some of the ways you deal with problems in a client's employment history?

People pursuing jobs in the $30,000 to $40,000 salary range are typically the group with negative information in their employment history that needs to be dealt with effectively in a resume. When someone has negative information or a lack of work experience, I tend to focus on creating a skill-based resume.

In this situation, the skill headings used within the resume become extremely important. I recommend that someone who needs a skill-based resume find at least five to ten help-wanted ads for job openings they'd be interested in filling. By reviewing those ads, the job seeker should be able to create a comprehensive list of skills to focus on within their resume.

There is no point in highlighting skills you know the employer has little or no interest in. So, by evaluating help-wanted ads, you can pinpoint the skills in demand and that will make you more marketable. It's these skills that should be highlighted within your resume.

Once someone hires you, how quickly will he or she receive a resume that's ready to submit to a potential employer?

A lot depends on how quickly the client responds to the list of questions I provide them with. The whole process can be done in a matter of days. Most clients don't realize how in-depth the questions are that I ask, so it takes them several days or a week to think about and then compile their answers.

Do you target a client's resume to each potential employer he or she contacts?

I can target a resume; however, most of my clients take my resume and are able to make small edits in order to customize it for each job they apply for. If someone is applying for several jobs that are very different, that's when it is most important to create truly customized resumes for each of those jobs. I tend to focus the resumes I create to a specific area, since I don't believe general resumes are worthwhile.

Do you offer a guarantee?

I personally don't offer a guarantee, mainly because I don't have to. On my website, I offer over 30 testimonials from clients. I have visited many websites promoting other peoples' resume-creation services. The guarantees they offer are often meaningless.

No matter how good someone's resume is, you can't guarantee it will land them a job or even get them called in for an interview. A resume writer can certainly help improve someone's chances of impressing a potential employer, however.

What is the biggest misconception job seekers have about profes-sional resume writers?

I know my clients are always surprised about how many questions I ask them before I actually begin writing their resume. Some people think they can pay someone to create their resume, but have no involvement in providing content for it. Some resume writers simply make a point to use verbose language to make a resume seem more impressive. I don't believe that's the best approach. I create resumes that contain truthful facts in a way that captures the reader's attention.

When people create their own resumes, what are some of the biggest mistakes you see them make?

People don't promote the best of what they have to offer within their resume, and they're not even aware of it. Most job seekers can't see the forest for the trees when it comes to creating content for a resume. As a result, they don't promote themselves as being as qual-ified as they possibly can for a position.

Another mistake is that people don't choose the best resume format to meet their individual needs. If you choose to use a traditional chronological formatted resume, each previous job you've held should help convey that you're qualified for the job you're applying for.

Conveying the right job titles and describing your responsibilities in past jobs are also areas where job seekers tend to make mistakes. Not many job seekers properly showcase their skills within their resume.

How important is using keywords as opposed to action verbs within a resume?

Anytime you're going to post your resume online or you know the resume will be scanned into a database, using keywords is the only way a potential employer is going to find you in the database. But, most people still need to have a paper resume for their interview. In this type of resume, using action verbs is critical in order to make your information read properly.

Most people these days need to have two versions of their resume—a paper resume with action verbs, and an electronic resume that uses keywords. Many resume writers will charge extra for creating two types of resumes, but for most job seekers, the additional investment will be well worth it, depending on the types of jobs you're applying for. When creating a keyword-based resume, I typically try to incorporate at least 50 keywords into the document.

Do you have any other advice for a job seeker looking to hire a professional resume writer?

If you take the time yourself to write down solid information for the person you hire to create your resume, the final document you will receive back will be that much better. Providing good job descriptions in advance for past employment experiences, for example, will ultimately save you money because it will take the resume writer less time to gather and process this information before incorporating it into your resume.

If you have already created your own resume and you're receiving a high response rate from potential employers, yet you're not landing any jobs, the problem is most likely with your interviewing skills, not your resume. If, however, you're sending out resumes and receiving a very low response rate, say under 40 or 50%, or the job offers you're receiving based on your resume aren't within the salary range you know you're qualified to earn, then chances are there's something about your resume that needs improvement.

Is there any other piece of advice you can offer to someone looking to hire a professional resume writer?

Yes. Seeing if the person you want to hire is certified is always helpful, but even if they are certified, still ask the important questions before hiring them. Ask to see samples of their work, as well as letters of recommendation from past clients. Just because someone promotes themselves as being certified, it doesn't necessarily mean they're good at what they do.

When considering whether or not to spend a few hundred dollars to have your resume professionally written, think about the income you're losing during the time you're not employed. If having your resume professionally written will help you land a higher-paying job faster, than you're actually saving money, not spending it.

the 35 resume
mistakes to avoid

ALTHOUGH THERE ARE countless errors someone can make when creating a resume, at least 35 are extremely common. Despite the fact that many of these errors seem obvious as you read them, a huge percentage of job seekers just like you lose out on excellent job opportunities due to carelessness or laziness.

Great Idea!

"Be sure to clearly include all your contact information in your heading. If a potential employer cannot easily figure out where to reach you, he or she might just forget about you."

—SANDY, EDITOR

Once your resume is complete, review this list carefully, then proofread your resume to ensure yours doesn't contain one of the errors that could easily result in it getting filed in the circular bin known as the wastebasket. Even if you are an extremely qualified candidate, most HR professionals and people responsible for hiring others make a point to discard resumes that contain careless mistakes, simply because it demonstrates poor attention to details on the the applicant's part.

The job-search process is extremely stressful and time-consuming. If you're not willing to take the extra steps needed to ensure that you are making every effort to showcase yourself and your qualifications in the best way, why should an employer hire you?

Great Idea!

"Make sure to target your resume to the specific job you are applying for. If the hiring manager cannot find a clear objective that relates to the job, he or she may pass over your resume for someone who put in the extra time to clearly state an objective."

—Ian, Consultant

In addition to proofreading your own resume, to ensure you haven't made any of the errors on this list, be sure to also recruit a friend, relative, or someone else to proofread your work (including your resume, cover letter, and any other written correspondence between yourself and the potential employer).

The following is a list of 35 of the most common mistakes job seekers make, as well as advice on how you can avoid them. This list is in no particular order, because making these mistakes has a similar negative result when read by an employer.

1. **A typographical or grammatical error in a resume is one of the worst mistakes you can make.** If you refuse to take the time to proofread your resume, why should an employer assume you will take the needed time to do your job properly if hired? There are many ways to ensure your resume is error-free. If you've

created your resume using word processing or resume-creation software, be sure to use the spell checker. Next, proofread your resume carefully. Finally, ask someone else to proofread your resume.

2. **Spelling mistakes are probably the most common resume mistakes.** These can easily be avoided, yet virtually all HR professionals say that the majority of resumes they receive contain at least one spelling error. A spelling mistake on your resume demonstrates carelessness and a lack of attention to detail. That's not the message you want to send to employers.

3. **Avoid stretching the truth.** A growing number of employers are verifying all resume information. If you're caught lying, you won't be offered a job, or you could be fired later if it's discovered that you weren't truthful. Lying or misrepresenting your qualifications can lead to disaster. There are multiple ways to handle gaps in your resume as well as negative information in your employment history. Lying, however, should never be considered.

4. **As part of your resume's heading, don't forget to list your full name, address, telephone number, e-mail address, and personal website (if you have one).** Starting with your full name at the top of the page, your contact information should be the first piece of information someone reading your resume sees. They should not have to spend more than a few seconds determining who you are and how to contact you.

5. **If an employer can't easily reach you to invite you for an interview or offer you a job, chances are another applicant will be selected, even if you're totally qualified.** Make sure people can reach you easily by listing a phone number on your resume that's connected to an answering machine or has a 24-hour answering service. Don't rely on someone to take messages for you. Listing a pager number or cell phone number on your resume is an option if this will make it easier for a potential employer to contact you.

6. Because most people look for new employment while still employed (and job seekers want to keep their job search a

secret), **never list your current work phone number or e-mail address at work on your resume.** It's easy for your current employer to discover that you're looking for new employment if you start receiving calls or e-mail from other potential employers while at work. If, however, you're being downsized or your current employer is going out of business, it's usually more acceptable to be less secretive about your job search.

7.   The visual appearance of your traditional printed resume is as important as its content. Choose one easy-to-read, 12-point font, such as Times Roman, New Century Schoolbook, or Garamond. **Don't mix and match multiple fonts.** Also, refrain from overusing **bold text,** underlining, *italic typestyles,* or mixing font sizes. A good resume is one that's easy to read and pleasing to the eye. Too many people try to use more than one or two fonts, combined with **bold text,** *italics,* and under-lining scattered throughout their resume. (As you can see, this makes text look busier and less friendly to the eye.) The result is a document that's confusing to read and look at.

8.   If you're applying for a traditional job, **don't include clip art or graphic images within your resume.** This is only appropriate if you're hoping to land a job as an artist, or plan to work in an industry such as advertising, where employers are looking for creativity. Also, refrain from adding a photo of yourself to your resume.

9.   As you've already read within this book, there are several different resume formats from which to choose to convey information to potential employers. Although most people will use a chronological resume format, a functional resume or a targeted/combination resume is better suited for people changing careers, trying to cover up large employment gaps, or for people who want to take attention away from negative information in their employment history. These other formats are also useful to someone with little or no previous work experience. **Using an uncommon resume format (anything but the chronological resume format) can be both beneficial and detrimental, however.** Although using an alternate

resume format can highlight your strengths, any HR professional who typically receives chronological resumes will certainly notice a different resume format and might assume the use of a different format is to hide negative information instead of highlighting positive information.

10. **Refrain from including any references to your past earning history (salary) or how much you're looking to earn.** Compensation can be discussed in a job interview situation once you're offered the job or the employer expresses a strong interest in hiring you.

11. **Never include on your resume or cover letter the reasons why you stopped working for an employer, switched jobs, or are currently looking for a new job.** If necessary, this information can be discussed later, during an interview. Don't include a line in your resume saying, "Unemployed" or "Out of Work" along with the corresponding dates in order to fill a time gap in a chronological resume. If there's negative information or a gap in your employment history, you should discuss this in person with a potential employer during an interview situation. This allows you to put a positive spin on the information.

12. **Frequent job hopping is something employers don't look favorably upon.** Because it's expensive to train new employees, few employers are willing to invest in someone with a record of jumping between jobs frequently. Someone who can demonstrate a sense of loyalty to their past employer will be more desirable.

    The good news is that the traditional approach to a career—which used to be to stay with one company for decades, if not for your entire career—is no longer expected. Most companies now realize that employees move from one company to another more frequently. So as long as you stay at a job and a company for a reasonable amount of time (which could be a year or two), employers no longer perceive this as frequent job hopping, but a desire to move quickly to a desired level and to get ahead.

13. **Instead of using long paragraphs to describe past work experience, consider using a bulleted list.** Most employers spend

less than one minute initially reading a resume, so it's critical that key information, such as work experience, is easy to find and is described with descriptive and punchy action words and phrases. Avoid using too much technical jargon (which is different from including keywords and phrases in your resume that describe specific jobs or responsibilities). Someone in an HR department might not understand technical jargon associated with your particular job, especially if it's a technical one, but that same HR person will look for specific words, job titles, or phrases within your resume. Using keywords is particularly important if your resume is going to be scanned into applicant-tracking software.

14. **Print your resume and cover letter on the same type of paper, and use matching envelopes to create synergy throughout your resume package.** Avoid brightly colored paper or cheap 20-pound copy paper. Visit any stationery or office-supply store to purchase quality resume paper. Be prepared to spend between 15¢ and $1.00 per sheet of resume paper (a bit less if you purchase packages of matching paper and envelopes). Bright white or cream-colored resume paper is the most popular. These colors also work best with applicant-tracking software if the employers you submit your resume to scan it into their systems. Use 24- or 28-pound bond paper made of 100% cotton stock. Using paper with a watermark is optional and a matter of personal taste.

15. Once you choose your resume paper, select an ink color. Avoid wild colors and mixing multiple colors. **Black ink is the most popular and most traditional color.** If you choose to print your resume using an alternate color ink, make sure your selection is professional looking. Brown or burgundy are good alternatives. Make sure the ink color and the paper you choose don't clash. Also, make sure the text is easily readable both to the human eye and to computer scanners. If faxing your resume to employers, your paper and ink color selections should be white paper with black ink. If your resume is difficult to read, people won't read it.

16. **Never send photocopies of your resume.** This is highly unprofessional. Use a laser printer to generate copies of your resumes from a computer or have it professionally typeset and printed.

17. **Don't staple your resume to a cover letter or fold it.** If mailing your resume to a potential employer, use a large envelope. One of the reasons why this is important is because wrinkles in your resume (or staples) make it difficult for a company to scan your resume into applicant-tracking software. If your resume doesn't scan properly, your chances of being considered for a position diminish dramatically.

18. Don't waste words. Every line or sentence in your resume should say something important and specific about you, your educational background, your work history, or your accomplishments. **All sentences and bulleted points should be short and to the point.** Your sentences should be under 20 words each, and all paragraphs should be ten lines or less. Remove redundant words and phrases.

19. **Use an impersonal voice.** Many resume-creation experts recommend removing pronouns (such as I, you, he, she, it, or they) from your resume. Statements such as "I managed an office of 20 people" or "I was responsible for boosting sales 35% in one year" can make you appear arrogant. **Instead, write your resume taking an impersonal approach.** For example, the statement "Responsible for boosting sales 35% in one year" has a much better tone. Don't waste the reader's time providing him or her with irrelevant information.

20. **Don't emphasize keywords if you're creating a traditional printed resume; focus on using action verbs and descriptive phrases.** This adds more power to your resume. Refrain from using clichés (overused phrases or words), such as "hard working." Use a thesaurus or the list of action verbs/phrases supplied at the end of this book, and find creative and powerful ways to communicate your main points.

21. **Aside from careless mistakes in a resume, one of the biggest reasons a qualified candidate often gets passed over for a job**

is because the resume wasn't targeted to the position for which they were applying. A resume can either be too broad or not specifically targeted to a job. If after someone reads your resume, he or she can't immediately conclude that you're a qualified candidate for the specific job for which you're applying, then your resume isn't serving its purpose, and you should rewrite it. Ideally, you want to specifically target your resume for each job for which you apply. This means using the same job titles and descriptive words and phrases used by the employer to describe the job opening in the ad or job listing.

22. **Don't include personal information unless it sets you apart from the crowd.** Some people choose to put personal information about themselves at the bottom of their resume. For example, they list hobbies or special skills that don't directly relate to the job for which they're applying. Unless each piece of information on your resume specifically showcases you as an ideal candidate, refrain from including it. For example, if you're applying for a bookkeeping position at a medium-size company, listing that your favorite hobby is deep-sea fishing is irrelevant. At the same time, you want to demonstrate, through your resume, that you're a well-rounded person with skills and experience that the employer may find useful. One possible exception to this rule is if you know your company has an active softball team or the employees often participate in a specific recreational activity together, such as golf. Then, you might want to mention you're an active participant in that sport or activity. If you have won competitions, awards, or other recognition in a sport or hobby, you might want to include that. This can easily be done, however, during an interview and doesn't necessarily need to be mentioned on your resume.

23. Don't include fluff in your educational background and previous work experience. Although you want to list specific accomplishments achieved while on the job in each position you've held, **avoid including information that's unimpressive, unimportant, or that won't be of direct interest to a**

potential employer. Instead, focus on the skills, accomplishments, and personality traits for which you know the employer is looking.

24. It's easy to make vague or generic statements about yourself and your professional accomplishments on your resume. Make your statements concrete, and support them with quantitative information as well as qualitative information. **Provide back-up support for the statements you make on your resume.** For example, if you list a sales manager position, mention your achievements during the time you held that job. Making a statement that as sales manager, you managed a salesforce of ten people and that your previous employer's sales rose 22% in six months demonstrates you held a position of responsibility and generated results.

25. **As you're writing your resume, don't forget to focus on the general skills for which you know the majority of employers are looking.** You definitely want to demonstrate at least some computer literacy and your ability to work well with others. Emphasize teamwork on your resume, focusing on leadership or managerial positions you've held in order to demonstrate you can take charge of a situation or a group of people. These are traits employers look for, and failure to demonstrate them could result in your missing a good job opportunity.

26. Don't make it hard to find information. **Make sure the sections of your resume are clearly defined.** The main sections of a resume are the: Heading, Job Objectives, Education, Accreditation and Licenses, Skills, Work and Employment Experience, Professional Affiliations, Military Service, References, and Personal Information. Choose what information about yourself should be included under each of the headings. The actual wording for each resume section can be modified. Also, only include the sections that apply to you.

27. **Don't clutter your resume.** One mistake too many people make is leaving in too much extraneous information. Keep your resume short and simple. Try to use simple words, and begin sentences with action verbs.

28. **Don't overlook an opportunity because of an unfamiliar job title.** Many industries use their own set of job titles. For example, Internet-based companies typically hire web designers, web developers, web content creators, or site managers as opposed to traditional graphic artists. If you're a graphic artist looking to work for an Internet company, make sure you describe your skills as a graphic artist, but also mention your proficiency using the programming languages and software tools commonly used in the industry, such as Shockwave, Director, PhotoShop, Illustrator, Java, and HTML.

29. **Never plagiarize a sample resume you find in a book or simply insert your own name and contact information.** Although this book doesn't offer a large collection of sample resumes, many other how-to resume-writing books on the market do. Sample resumes are designed to provide you with formatting guidelines and advice on how to promote your achievements within your resume.

30. Try not to send a resume not addressed to an individual. To ensure that the resume you submit to a potential employer actually gets read (or reviewed), **be sure to address it to a specific person within a company.** Make sure the person's full name is spelled correctly and that you use his or her job title both on the envelope and in your cover letter. The chances of your resume getting read are greatly reduced if you send it blind.

31. Don't use the wrong type of resume. In addition to several popular resume formats, there are three basic types of resumes: traditional printed resumes, electronic (digital) resumes, and scannable resumes. **Make sure you know what type of resume you're trying to create.** A scannable resume, for example, is one that's printed on paper, but that's designed to be scanned into applicant-tracking software and initially evaluated by a computer as opposed to a person. An electronic (digital) resume is one sent via e-mail, posted on the Web, or otherwise distributed electronically.

32. If you're an accomplished professional, **make sure your most important accomplishments aren't lost in your resume.** Choose several of your greatest achievements and make sure they're highlighted and won't be missed by someone glancing at your resume for ten to fifteen seconds.

33. As you write your resume, especially one targeted to a specific employer (for a specific job opening), make sure the contents of your resume target the specific needs and concerns of the employer. **Don't just modify the "Objective" section of your resume.** If necessary, edit your entire resume so it caters to the needs of a specific employer for which you'd like to work. Obviously, creating a targeted resume involves a bigger time commitment and a better understanding of a company's needs, but this is one of the best ways to capture the attention of a potential employer—especially one for which you would really want to work. A targeted resume is more likely to capture someone's attention than a generic one sent to dozens of employers.

34. **Don't include references to your age on your resume.** In today's business world, ageism remains a common problem. If you're perceived to be too young or too old for a position, you might not be considered. Thus, your resume should offer little or no hint of your age. Using a chronological formatted resume makes it possible for an employer to calculate your approximate age based on the number of years you've been working, but this requires work on the part of the employer. You do not even need to mention your graduation date (which is an obvious way to calculate the age of most candidates, unless you graduated later than usual). If a company requires your college transcript, they will let you know—and if they do, it means the company is seriously considering you, so you've probably already met with an HR or hiring manager who will know roughly how old you are, so your age will matter less.

35. Finally, if your resume does not answer the following questions, it needs to be rewritten:
    - What skills do you offer to the organization?
    - Are you worth the salary you're hoping to earn? Do you offer at least that much value to the employer?
    - How can you help the company face its current challenges, overcome obstacles, or achieve greater success?

CHAPTER 11

putting the pieces together and landing a job

ONCE YOU SET a career path and acquire the education, skills, and experience you need to pursue your professional goals, your resume and cover letter will allow you to make that all-important first impression with employers as you begin applying for jobs.

Hopefully, as you've been reading *Resumes That Get You Hired*, you've developed an understanding of why having a powerful and well-written resume is important. You should also now have the knowledge needed to create a resume that will capture an employer's attention and showcase you as the ideal candidate for the job(s) for which you choose to apply.

Aside from your resume and cover letter, many other components to your overall job-search efforts require attention before actually receiving your first paycheck after landing a new job. Assuming your resume and cover letter achieve their objectives, you will be invited to participate in job interviews and will need to complete employment applications.

Throughout this entire process, you need to keep track of contacts and appointments, make important career-related decisions, evaluate job offers; and if you're like most job seekers, deal with rejection. After all, not everyone receives the first job for which they apply.

This chapter helps you deal with some of the other aspects of the job-search process, once you've written a resume and cover letter(s). As you embark on this whole process, take an organized approach and don't let the stress get to you. Also, don't underestimate the value and marketability of your skills and experience and settle for a job where you will be underutilized and underpaid.

By carefully evaluating each job offer you receive and by making well-thought-out decisions based on research, you will be able to find a job that pays you what you deserve, that offers upward mobility, and that you will enjoy.

Whatever happens, don't settle for a dead-end job simply because you want or need a paycheck. Far too many people get caught up in jobs they hate and wind up miserable. Having a job you dislike will have a major impact on your personal and professional life. In most cases, it's easy to avoid winding up in a job that you will hate.

Instead of quickly accepting the first job offer you receive, simply because you need money, during your job search, consider working for a temp agency and taking temporary work assignments. This will ensure you have a paycheck coming in during your job-search efforts and will give you the freedom to take a bit longer to find the perfect job opportunity. Working temp jobs can also be used as a networking opportunity to meet other

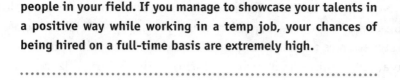

people in your field. If you manage to showcase your talents in a positive way while working in a temp job, your chances of being hired on a full-time basis are extremely high.

ARE YOU EARNING WHAT YOU'RE WORTH?

Are you like most people, working too hard, for too many hours per week, yet not getting paid what you believe you deserve? Due to ever-increasing competition, employers often push employees to work longer hours and assume more responsibilities yet offer less pay. Because salaries and compensation packages are typically kept confidential within a company, it can be difficult to determine if you're getting paid what you deserve based on your experience, skills, education, and overall value to the company for which you work.

Whether you're looking for a new job, hoping to earn a raise, or you're convinced you're not getting paid what you're worth in your current job, you can do several things to discover your own true earning potential.

Many things contribute to someone's salary and overall compensation package. Work experience, education, skills, the size of the company, the industry, the employer's geographic location, demand, the number of hours you work, and your ability to negotiate the best possible salary/compensation package all help to determine what you get paid.

Once you know exactly what type of job you're looking to fill (or that you currently fill), by performing research, you can determine what salary range someone holding a similar job title and responsibilities earns within your industry and geographic area. Using this information, you can then determine if you're currently earning less than what you're worth and take the necessary steps to either pursue a higher-paying job or a raise.

No matter what industry in which you are employed, it's possible to pinpoint average salaries paid by employers for specific jobs. One of the best resources for gathering current and accurate salary information (available online or in printed form) is the Salary Wizard™ from www.Salary.com, which allows you to search—free—average salary information by job title (and level), either by national average or specific to a particular U.S. city. The site provides a salary range (for base pay), the median salary, and additional information on a total compensation package (which would include the dollar value of possible bonuses, benefits—including Social Security, 401(k)/403(b), disability, healthcare, pension, and time off—and the net paycheck estimate), as well as other useful information.

Another traditional source of information is the *Occupational Outlook Handbook* (www.bls.gov/oco). The *Occupational Outlook Handbook* is available at most libraries; the career services office at most high schools, colleges, and universities; as well as online. It can also be ordered for $64 by calling 202-512-1800. For each of the thousands of occupations covered, this directory describes the nature of the work, working conditions, employment opportunities, the job outlook (between 1998 and 2008), the earning potential/salary range, as well as information about related occupations.

The Web contains many research firms and other sources of salary information, but when using these sources for research, it's important to determine from where this information is derived, whether or not it's current, and if the data applies to your industry, occupation, and geographic area.

JobSmart (www.jobsmart.org/tools/salary/sal-prof) is a free service that publishes more than 300 profession-specific salary surveys online for professions ranging from accounting to warehousing and by geographic region.

The Clayton Wallis Company's CompGeo Online service (707-996-0967, www.claytonwallis.com) offers online information about salaries based on geographic location. For example, if you're working in healthcare, you can determine what people with your qualifications earn around the country using the information offered at this website. CompGeo offers salary information for over 1,200 job classifications.

Salary Master is an independent company that represents IT professionals during salary negotiations. The company's website (www.salarymaster.com) offers a collection of articles and information for people looking to determine what they're worth as an employee in a high-tech field.

If you're contemplating moving to another city, you can easily compare what you're earning in one city with what you could be making in another doing the same type of work by visiting Yahoo!'s Salary Comparison website at verticals.yahoo.com/salary.

Through research, it's relatively easy to determine if you're getting paid less than what you're worth in today's marketplace. Knowing exactly what you're worth helps you participate successfully in salary negotiation with your current or future employer.

During the negotiation process, always let the employer make the first offer. Once an offer is made, never accept it on the spot. Tell the employer you need at least several hours or a full day to consider the offer. If you know an employer is doing well financially and is desperate to fill the position you're qualified to fill, you will have the advantage in a salary negotiation.

Never use your personal financial situation as a reason for requesting more money. Comments like "I need more money to afford my mortgage, rent, or car payments" do not concern the employer. Instead, focus on the *value* you offer the company and be prepared to offer qualitative and quantitative information to support your statements. Your chances of receiving the salary you're seeking increases dramatically by proving to an employer you're worth it.

If you've never participated in a salary negotiation, read a book on how to negotiate so you become familiar with various tactics employers use during the salary negotiation process (for example, LearningExpress's *Job Interviews That Get You Hired* covers negotiating). Never settle for earning less than what you know you deserve based on your research. Keep in mind, however, there's a big difference between earning what you're worth in today's marketplace and what you think you're worth.

TAKING A DEADLINE-ORIENTED
APPROACH TO LANDING A JOB

Landing a job is often a confusing, stressful, and extremely time-consuming task. You have to find job opportunities, create a resume, write cover letters, schedule interviews, perform research on companies, participate in interviews, make follow-up calls, and keep track of all the potential employers with which you meet or correspond. One way to avoid the stress of this whole procedure is to adopt an organized, deadline-oriented approach to finding a job.

Begin by acquiring a personal planner, such as a Day-Timer, or a personal digital assistant (PDA), such as the Palm Pilot III, V, or VII. Before actually starting your job search, make a list of everything you will need to accomplish to land a job. Break down the big task into lots of smaller ones, which are easier to accomplish. If you have to write or update your resume, add it to your list. If you need to buy outfits to wear to interviews, that too goes on your list. Once your list is complete, write down how long you think each task will take to accomplish.

Next, prioritize your list. Determine what tasks need to be done immediately and which ones can wait until later in the job-search process. Now that you know what you need to do and approximately how long it will take to accomplish each task, create a schedule for yourself and set deadlines.

Using your personal planner, calendar, or PDA, start at today's date and enter in each job-search-related task, one at a time. Under your list of tasks to complete, add items like "check the help-wanted ads" and "update resume." Leave yourself enough time to accomplish each task, and in your planner, mark down the date by which each task should be completed.

Keep meticulous notes in your planner or on your PDA. Write down everything you do, with whom you make contact, the phone numbers and addresses of your contacts, what is discussed on the phone or during interviews, and what follow-up actions need to be taken. Throughout your job-search process, keep your planner or PDA with you at all times. Refer to it and update it often to ensure that you remain on track.

To demonstrate that you are a well-organized person, refer to your planner or PDA during job interviews, and don't be afraid to make notes during the interview. If a potential employer wants to schedule a second interview, take out your planner or PDA, and schedule an appointment on the spot.

A personal planner, such as a Day-Timer, costs between $15 and $110, and provides you with places to write down appointments, to-do lists, expenses, and other information. Different formats of personal planners are available, allowing you to view one day, multiple days, a week, or even a month at a time. You can also include an address book in your planner, and keep all your information in one handy place.

Personal digital assistants (also called electronic organizers) cost more money, between $50 and $1,000, because they're essentially hand-held computers. PDAs have built-in electronic scheduling programs, address books, to-do lists, and some even have word processors or text editors, all packed into a hand-held unit that can be taken anywhere. PDAs are ideal tools for people looking for a job, because they can hold vast amounts of information in an organized manner.

Once you land a job, don't toss out your personal planner or organizer. Writing what you need to accomplish, prioritizing those tasks, setting deadlines for yourself, and keeping this information with you will help you stay focused, save time, and avoid procrastination.

To find a personal planner or PDA that meets your needs, visit any office-supply store. Getting into the habit of using an organizational tool will take some getting used to, so stick with it. You will soon experience the benefits of being a better organized, deadline-oriented person, which all employers value.

DON'T LET REJECTION GET YOU DOWN

So, you got invited for a job interview, you thought everything went well and that the employer loved you, but you later discovered that someone else was hired to fill the position. Does this mean you're a failure? Should you take this rejection personally? The answer to these questions is *no*!

Unfortunately, rejection is part of the overall job-search process, and it's something with which you have to deal. If you don't land a job you want, don't waste time or energy getting angry with the employer. Instead, learn as much as you can from the experience and move on. If you're absolutely certain that the job you didn't receive is the ideal one for you, there's nothing stopping you from re-applying, or applying for a different position within the same company, with the plan of eventually transferring into the position you want.

As you embark upon the job-search process, several things can help increase your chances for landing a job. First, apply only for jobs for which you're qualified. Never lie on your resume or during an interview to appear more qualified. Next, just because you find one job opening that grabs your interest, don't stop sending resumes and scheduling other interviews. That age-old saying, "Don't put all of your eggs in one basket," applies.

Should you find yourself rejected for multiple jobs for similar reasons, consider adjusting your job-search approach. Perhaps you should edit your resume to give it more focus. Maybe you're coming on too strong or not strong enough during interviews. Never start playing what-if mind games with yourself or stressing over actions you've already taken. Instead, focus all of your job search energies on the future: toward finding and landing a job you will truly enjoy and for which you will be totally qualified.

Don't feel like you're alone. Richard Leger, director of career services at Boston University stated, "What I tell my students is: Always be sure that you have an individual that you can discuss everything you're doing with and that can offer you guidance. Make sure that the person will be totally honest with you. This person should also be older, or someone with more experience with the job search process. Ideally, a career counselor is the best person to give you guidance and honest appraisals."

A career counselor can help you stay focused and determine why you're being rejected, and then work with you to rectify the situation. "Never personalize the job hunt. What most people do is personalize rejection and consider themselves a failure, instead of believing that they simply didn't fit the job they applied for. Receiving rejection can be like a virus and build up inside you if you don't deal with it correctly. Don't dwell on your weaknesses. Know what your strengths are, work with them and communicate them, and then let the whole process evolve based on your strengths," added Leger.

Finally, go into every job interview totally prepared, having done your research, knowing what position you want and why you're qualified for it, and having prepared a list of intelligent questions to ask the employer. Applicants who are totally prepared automatically develop a sense of confidence and become far less nervous. Thus, it's usually these people who make the best impressions and appear the most qualified. Making sure you're qualified for a job and being totally prepared for the interview are two things you can do to greatly increase your chances of landing a job and avoid rejection.

COMPLETING JOB APPLICATIONS

Most employers require applicants to complete a job application prior to an interview. An application is a questionnaire that takes a few minutes to complete, but it's a useful tool for helping employers evaluate you as an applicant.

Job seekers often complete their applications by hand. The completed application demonstrates how well you communicate on paper and how legible your handwriting is, shows whether or not you can spell and use proper punctuation, summarizes the information in your resume, and provides the employer with a list of your references. Thus, what you write on an application, in addition to how you write it, impacts an employer's decision about hiring you.

For each question on the application, think carefully about how you can answer it concisely and accurately. As you complete the actual application, neatly print all of your answers using a blue or black ballpoint pen. Avoid writing in script, crossing out mistakes, or using more space than provided. Don't use any words you don't know how to spell. Employers will look for answers that are written in complete sentences, using proper English.

Most applications ask you to fill in the position for which you're applying and list what salary you're looking to earn. Use the exact wording that was listed in the help-wanted ad or listing to which you responded. As for desired salary, instead of providing an actual figure, write "negotiable." Encourage the employer to make the first offer regarding salary.

When you fill in your educational background, remember that employers will likely contact the educational institution you claim to have attended, so list only degrees or diplomas you have actually earned.

Many applications request that you write a paragraph listing any skills, research work, areas of interest, or special training you have. Refer to your resume and ensure the information you provide is consistent. Also, try to incorporate action words into your descriptions to add impact.

Providing references is another key component to virtually all job applications. Prior to listing anyone's name and contact information, check with the people you want to list, and obtain their permission to use them as references. Also, ask what address and phone number you should provide to potential employers, because some people don't like having their home phone number or direct office line given out. Be sure to tell the people you use as a reference exactly what position you're applying for, so they will be prepared if one of your potential employers contacts them.

Never include an immediate family member as a reference. Employers don't consider relatives or best friends to be credible references. Previous employers and coworkers, prominent business people in the community who know you, former professors, and leaders of charity groups for whom you've done volunteer work all make excellent references.

At the end of every application, you will be asked to sign a statement that the information provided is accurate to the best of your knowledge. Later, if an employer discovers you've provided false information, you could be fired.

By following all directions on the application, writing neatly, providing accurate and well-thought-out answers using complete sentences, and highlighting your skills and accomplishments in the space provided, you will be one step closer to landing whatever job you apply for.

SELL YOURSELF USING MORE THAN A TRADITIONAL RESUME

Throughout this book, you've been advised to keep your resume short and concise. This allows a potential employer to quickly grasp your qualifications. When you sit down to write a resume, however, you will soon realize that you can't always convey all the information you believe is important within this limited space.

Still, you have to keep in mind that the person reading your resume is probably extremely busy. Providing him or her with too much information initially won't work in your favor. Job seekers must develop strategies to convey additional information that can't be crammed into the traditional one-page resume format.

Information to Include in Your Cover Letter

Your cover letter is one of the best ways to convey important facts about your career and highlight specific achievements directly related to the job you're seeking. Like a resume, your cover letter should be kept short. It's useful, however, to include details that aren't listed within your resume, or to elaborate on items—mentioning specific facts or figures can work in your favor.

The cover letter should focus on aspects of your education, work history, or skills that will most interest the potential employer. It should focus on what you can do for the employer and describe some of your personal qualities as well as your specific skills, all using upbeat wording.

For example, you might describe yourself as a highly motivated, well-organized, detail-oriented person capable of managing others. Once you make a statement like this, you will need to provide supporting evidence by describing a specific accomplishment from your employment history. Make a statement like, "In my previous job, I managed a salesforce of nine people, and sales for the year rose 25% due to the unique sales strategies and materials I created and implemented."

How Letters of Recommendation Can Help

Another option is providing letters of recommendation, which may enhance your credibility, especially if the letters are written by previous employers or people known to the potential employer.

Letters of recommendation should showcase your individual skills or desirable qualities. For example, a letter from a previous boss describing your dedication, perfect attendance record, and several specific achievements on the job will be impressive to any reader. Strong and truthful statements from previous employers always enhance your chances of getting hired.

A letter of recommendation from a previous boss that states, "Thanks to her hard work, leadership ability, and dedication as our sales manager, last year our company's sales grew 20%. I believe (applicant's name) will be an asset to any company she chooses to work for," will certainly help capture the reader's attention.

Some people include one or two letters of recommendation when initially sending their resume and cover letter to a potential employer. Others wait for their first in-person job interview to deliver these additional documents. Which option you choose can depend on your personal preference, how powerful the letters of recommendation are, who wrote the letters, how relevant they are to the job for which you're applying, and whether or not your resume and cover letter were solicited by the recipient. When responding to a help-wanted ad or sending an unsolicited resume, you want to keep your correspondence short, so it's probably best to wait and provide letters of recommendation during a job interview unless otherwise instructed.

Tips for Your Interview

You should also be prepared to convey specific details about your education, experience, and skills at your first in-person interview. Beforehand, decide what relevant information you hope to convey. It's perfectly acceptable to make notes to yourself and bring them into the interview, because it's common to forget important facts when you're nervous or under pressure.

Whereas your resume and cover letter are suitable for conveying general information about your employment history, education, skill set, and accomplishments, an in-person interview offers the perfect opportunity to elaborate on these facts. For example, if your resume states you were previously a sales manager at the ABC Company, during your interview, discuss your specific accomplishments, mentioning which skills you used on the job. Also, describe the results of your work in detail, and provide as much supporting evidence as possible.

Focus on how your skills and previous experience can benefit the potential employer. What value will you provide? How will your skills and work experience allow you to fulfill the responsibilities of the job for which you're applying? Why are you the perfect candidate to fill the position?

As you make statements about your career-related accomplishments or past employment experiences during an interview, provide support documentation. Start by reviewing details listed in your resume, and then elaborate by sharing other details about yourself and your career that a potential employer will find useful when making their hiring decision.

It's never appropriate to disclose classified documents from previous employers; however, any printed materials you can offer that corroborate what you tell a potential employer during an interview will add credibility to your statements.

If you previously received any type of award while on the job, such as Employee of the Month or Salesperson of the Year, offer documentation. Copies of company newsletters, reports that describe your accomplishments, and letters to you from past employers congratulating you on various achievements are all excellent support materials.

Providing potential employers with enough information about yourself so they can make educated hiring decisions is a skill that needs to be practiced and refined. In most circumstances, being able to convey additional information, aside from what's within your resume, will greatly improve your chances of being hired.

Preparing for a Job Interview

After sending your resumes and cover letters to potential employers, if you've done everything correctly, you should have at least a 50% success rate in terms of hearing back from potential employers and being invited to interview.

Job interviews are your time to shine as a person and sell yourself directly to the employer. Until now, you've used impersonal methods of communication to convey information about yourself. When you participate in an interview, your personality, appearance, charisma, knowledge, and body language help sell you as the perfect candidate for whatever job you're applying.

As part of your job interview preparation, think of the types of questions the interviewer might ask. Spend time developing well-thought-out, complete, and intelligent answers to these questions. Thinking about answers, or even writing answers on paper will be helpful, but what will benefit you the most is to practice answering interview questions aloud, and have someone you trust honestly evaluate your responses.

Great Idea!

"Appearance does count, even in today's business-casual world. Make sure to ask about the dress code when you're setting up the interview. Dress in a manner that makes you feel great. You want to exude confidence and capability. Do your homework and be prepared with questions to ask about the company. Research as much as possible regarding product line, services, markets, the competition, or whatever else you can find. It's not something that everyone does, and it helps set you apart and really shows people you are interested."

—CHRIS, CFO

Most of the questions you will be asked will be pretty obvious, but be prepared for an interviewer to ask you a few unexpected questions. By doing this, the interviewer wants to see how you react and how well you think on your feet.

As you answer all of the interviewer's questions, keep these guidelines in mind:

- Use complete sentences and proper English. Avoid using fillers such as "like," "umm," "you know," and so forth.
- Don't be evasive, especially if asked about negative aspects of your employment history.
- Never imply that a question is "stupid."
- Don't lie or stretch the truth.
- Be prepared to answer the same question multiple times. Make sure your answers are consistent, and never reply, "You already asked me that."
- Never apologize for negative information regarding your past.
- Avoid talking down to an interviewer, or making them feel less intelligent than you.

• • •

The following are common interview questions and suggestions on how you can best answer them:

1. *What can you tell me about yourself?*

   Emphasize your skills and accomplishments. Avoid talking about your family, hobbies, or topics not relevant to your ability to do the job.

2. *Why have you chosen to pursue your current career path?*

   Give specific reasons and examples.

3. *In your personal or professional life, what has been your greatest failure? What did you learn from that experience?*

   Be open and honest. Everyone has had some type of failure. Focus on what you learned from the experience and how it helped you to grow as a person.

4. *Why did you leave your previous job?*

   Try to put a positive spin on your answer, especially if you were fired for negative reasons. The company downsizing, going out of business, or some other reason that was out of your control is a perfectly acceptable answer. Remember, your answer will probably be verified.

5. *What would you consider to be your biggest accomplishments at your last job?*

   Talk about what made you a productive employee and a valuable asset to your previous employer. Emphasize that teamwork was involved in achieving your success, and that you work well with others.

6. *In college, I see you were a (insert subject) major. Why did you choose (insert subject) as your major?*

   Explain your interest in the subject matter, where that interest comes from, and how it relates to your current career-related goals.

7. *What are your long-term goals?*

   Talk about how you have been following a career path, and where you think this path will take you in the future. Describe how you believe the job for which you're applying is a logical step forward.

8. *Why do you think you're the most qualified person to fill this job?*

    Focus on the positive things that distinguish you from the competition. What's unique about you, your skill set, and past experiences? What work-related experience do you have that relates directly to this job?

9. *What have you heard about this company that was of interest to you?*

    Focus on the company's reputation. Refer to positive publicity, media attention, or published information that caught your attention. This shows you've done your research.

10. *What else can you tell me about yourself that isn't listed in your resume?*

    This is yet another opportunity for you to sell yourself to the employer. Take advantage of the opportunity.

Job Interviews: What *Not* to Do

Once you are invited by a potential employer for an interview, to maximize your chances of landing the job, it's critical to do everything within your power to prepare and avoid the common mistakes often made by applicants.

The following are some of the most common mistakes applicants make while preparing for or participating in job interviews, plus tips on how to avoid making these mistakes.

- **Never lie on a resume.** Don't apply for jobs for which you're not qualified and then lie to get invited for an interview.
- **Don't skip steps in your interview preparation.** Just because you've been invited for an interview, you can't afford to wing it once you get there. Prior to the interview, spend time doing research about the company, its products or services, and the people with whom you will meet.
- **Never arrive late for an interview.** Arriving even five minutes late for a job interview is equivalent to telling an

employer you don't want the job. If possible, the day before the interview, go to the interview location and determine exactly how to get there and how long it takes. On the day of the interview, plan on arriving at least 15 minutes early, and use the restroom before you begin the actual interview.

- **Don't neglect your appearance.** First impressions are crucial. Make sure your clothing is wrinkle-free and clean, that your hair is well groomed, and that your make-up (if applicable) looks professional. Always dress up for an interview, even if the dress code at the company is casual. Also, be sure to brush your teeth just before an interview, especially if you've recently eaten.

- **Avoid drinking any beverages containing caffeine.** Chances are, you will already be nervous about the interview. Drinking coffee or soda won't calm you down, so avoid them both before and during your interview. If your job interview takes place over lunch or dinner, refrain from drinking alcohol of any kind.

- **Don't go into the interview unprepared.** Beforehand, use your research to compile a list of intelligent questions to ask the employer. These questions can be about the company, its products or services, methods of doing business, the job responsibilities of the job for which you're applying, and so forth. When it's time for you to answer questions, always use complete sentences.

- **Never bring up salary, benefits, or vacation time during the initial interview.** Allow the employer to bring up the compensation package offered. Especially during the first interview, never bring up salary, benefits, or vacation time. Instead, focus on how you (with all of your skills, experience, and education) can become a valuable asset to the company with which you're interviewing.

- **Refrain from discussing your past earning history or what you're hoping to earn.** An employer typically looks for the best possible employees for the lowest possible price. Let the employer make you an offer first. When asked, tell the interviewer you're looking for a salary and benefits package that's in line with what's standard in the industry for someone with your qualifications and experience. Try to avoid stating an actual dollar figure.

- **During the interview, avoid personal topics.** There are questions that an employer can't legally ask during an interview or on an employment application. In addition to these topics, refrain from discussing sex, religion, politics, and any other highly personal topics.

- **Never insult the interviewer.** It's common for an interviewer to ask what you might perceive to be a stupid or irrelevant question. In some cases, the interviewer is simply testing to see how you will respond. Some questions are asked to test your morals or determine your level of honesty. Other types of questions are used simply to see how you will react in a tough situation. Try to avoid getting caught up in trick questions. Never tell an interviewer you think a question is stupid or irrelevant.

- **Throughout the interview, be aware of your body language.** For example, if you're someone who taps your foot when you're nervous, make sure you're aware of your habit so you can control it in an interview situation.

Throughout any job interview, your primary objective should be to position yourself as *the ideal candidate* for the job for which you're applying. Your chances of landing a job dramatically increase by avoiding the common mistakes made by many applicants.

One of the best ways to prepare for an interview is to participate in mock interviews with someone who will ask you questions and then honestly critique your responses.

WHEN JOB HUNTING, SHOW YOUR GRATITUDE

Unfortunately, the business world is a cut-throat environment. People often maintain a selfish, look-out-for-themselves attitude. When you are a job applicant, this is not the attitude to adopt. Many applicants believe that when they go on a job interview, the interviewer is simply doing his or her job by trying to fill the position their company has open. They believe that part of the interviewer's job is interviewing applicants, so the applicants offer no gratitude to the interviewer for their interest or for taking the time to meet with them. As a result of having this somewhat cynical attitude, many applicants never send a thank-you note after their interview—and that's a mistake.

"Many applicants don't send a thank-you note at all. Sending a personal and well-thought-out note immediately after an interview is extremely beneficial. It will keep your name in the forefront of the hiring manager's mind. It will also show that you have good follow-up skills and that you're genuinely interested in the job opportunity," explains Sue Nowacki, a partner at 1st Resumes, a full-service resume-writing firm (www.1stresumes.com).

The following are some basic steps to follow when writing and sending thank-you notes:

- Send individual and personalized thank-you notes, within 24 hours of your interview, to everyone you met with when visiting a potential employer. Send separate notes containing different messages to each person you met with.
- Address your thank-you note susing the recipient's full name and title. Make sure you spell the person's name correctly.
- Type, e-mail, or hand-write your note on personal stationery. If you choose to type your note, follow a standard business letter format. A much more personal alternative is to hand-write your thank you note on a professional-looking note card, which can be purchased at any stationery, greeting card, or office-supply store. The card should be white or cream colored with minimal ornamentation. Nowacki added, "The personal touch will add a lot to further a positive impression and help to separate you from your competition."
- Address the interviewer by title as Mr., Mrs., Ms., Dr. and last name in the salutation.

- Keep your message brief and to the point. Thank the interviewer for taking the time out of his or her busy schedule to meet with you, and for considering you for the available job opening. Make sure you include the exact job title or position for which you applied. In one or two sentences, highlight the important details discussed in your interview. You want the interviewer to remember you. Finally, reaffirm your interest in the position and invite further contact.
- Make sure your full name and phone number are included in the note.
- Do not mention issues under negotiation, such as salary, benefits, concerns, work schedule, etc. These subjects are not appropriate for a thank-you note.
- If possible, match the stationery or note card you use to your cover letter and resume paper. This helps you convey a uniform and well-thought-out image.

Just as your resume and cover letters are valuable job-search tools, think of the thank-you note as an extremely important follow-up tool, which has the potential of helping you to land the job.

Great Idea!

"Even if an employer likes an applicant, I know that many human resources professionals actually wait to see if they receive a thank-you note from an applicant before making a job offer. They also check the postmark to see how quickly after the interview the note was sent."

—SUE NOWACKI, PARTNER, 1ST RESUMES

As a job applicant, it's important to show your gratitude to *everyone* who helps you find and land a job. This includes the people you interview with, as well as any networking contacts who help you find job opportunities. If you demonstrate that you're grateful for people's help, they're more apt to keep helping you in the future. A thank-you note is a perfect and professional way to show your appreciation.

EMBARKING ON A JOB SEARCH WHILE STILL EMPLOYED

The best time to begin searching for new employment opportunities is while you are still employed. This eliminates a lot of the emotional and financial stress associated with having to land a job in order to obtain a paycheck. However, no matter what your reasons are for embarking on a new job search, it's important to show the proper respect toward your *current* employer, even if you consider yourself a disgruntled employee.

If your current position is being eliminated due to downsizing, layoffs, corporate restructuring, or another reason that's outside of your control, immediately inquire about the severance package to which you're entitled, obtain written letters of recommendation from your superiors, and take advantage of whatever career counseling services are offered.

In this type of situation, it's appropriate to be obvious about your job-search efforts and tap your networking skills to discover new employment opportunities. This may include contacting clients or customers, suppliers, or distributors with which your employer works, or anyone else outside your company you've had business dealings with as an employee. If given permission by the employer, it's also acceptable to take advantage of your employer's in-house resources, such as Internet access.

Many people choose to leave their current position because they're not happy in their present job, or perhaps it's possible to earn more money elsewhere. As someone who is currently employed but interested in exploring other job opportunities, you will probably want to keep your job search a secret.

As you'd expect, most employers frown upon employees soliciting or investigating other employment opportunities while on the job. As a result, finding time to go on job interviews when you're supposed to be at work may become a challenge. Likewise, you will probably find it difficult to call potential employers or receive calls from them and do research on potential employers when you're supposed to be working.

Especially if you're trying to keep your job-search efforts a secret, it is not acceptable to use your company's computers or Internet access to create your resume or surf the Web in search of new jobs, *especially* during normal business hours. Whether or not the computer you use at work is connected to a network, your activities can easily and legally be monitored by an employer, and your job-search efforts may easily be discovered.

Likewise, avoid using your employer's voice mail, fax machine, or e-mail address to correspond with potential new employers. Depending on your personal employment situation, there may also be legal or ethical issues in regards to making contact with your clients, customers, or other work-related contacts in order to find new job opportunities.

The best approach is to use a computer at home, on your own time, to create your resume and visit the career-related sites you're interested in. You should also have an answering machine or voice mail for your home phone, so if an employer calls while you're at work, you can call in for messages and return calls at your convenience.

If you don't have access to the Internet at home, you should still have (or obtain) a private e-mail address that can be accessed from any computer connected to the Web. Free e-mail addresses are available from services like Yahoo! (www.yahoo.com), MSN Hotmail (www.hotmail.com), and Excite (http://www.excite.com). E-mail sent to one of these addresses can be accessed from a friend or relative's computer, from a computer center at a school or library, or from any other PC that's not associated with your current employer.

One of the most difficult tasks you will face when searching for a job while still employed is finding time to go on interviews. Lying to your current employer by saying you have a doctor's appointment or need to run errands is one option. However, it's better to schedule interviews for mornings, evenings, or weekends, whenever possible.

When this can't be done, take advantage of your personal or vacation days, so you can take time off without having to reveal or misrepresent your whereabouts to your current employer.

As you explore new job opportunities, make it clear to potential employers that you'd appreciate them keeping your interest in their company confidential. Also, avoid responding to ads with blind P.O. boxes, where you don't know the name of the company you're sending your resume to. It's possible your current employer could be advertising those job opportunities, and you don't want to get caught applying for them!

Obviously, what you do on your own time, even if it includes searching for a new job, is your business. To avoid potential problems, however, don't allow your job-search efforts to interfere with your current job responsibilities. Also, when you ultimately land a new job, be prepared to give *at least* two weeks' notice to your current employer. Even if your new employer wants you to begin work immediately, it will usually respect your decision to give your current employer reasonable notice.

Finally, as you leave your current job, no matter how disappointed, angry, or frustrated, don't take anything that doesn't belong to you, such as office supplies, computer equipment, confidential files, or your company's client list. If you've signed a noncompetition or nondisclosure agreement with your current employer, have a lawyer review this document to ensure you won't get into trouble for accepting whatever new job is being offered.

People change jobs regularly. To eliminate much of the stress associated with keeping your job-search activities a secret, perform these activities on your own time, using your own resources.

A FEW LAST WORDS

By reading this book, you're now armed with the knowledge you need to create a powerful printed or electronic resume. To help you land a job faster, be sure to take full advantage of all of the resources available, and never be afraid to ask for assistance from friends,

family, former coworkers, former professors, career guidance counselors, a professional resume writer, or anyone else who might be
able to assist you in landing the job you want—a new position you
know you will enjoy!

Great Idea!

"When looking for a job, seek people first, then opportunity. Even if the job is in the perfect field and
requires your exact skills set, you will eventually dread
getting out of bed if you do not enjoy the people you
work closely with. In particular, as companies become
more project focused and fast paced, teams will be
increasingly important. Build your work around your
team, not your team around the work."

—JEREMY, SALES ASSOCIATE

A P P E N D I X **A**

action verbs and power phrases for your resume

AS YOU BEGIN to draft your traditional printed resume, you make a greater impact if you use action verbs to describe your accomplishments, skills, and responsibilities. Incorporate one action word for each item listed on your resume. As you incorporate these verbs into your resume, choose only the ones that work best with your individual skills and accomplishments, and refrain from using the same action verb two or more times. Even if you've held the same type of job with several different employers, use different wording to describe each of your employment experiences.

When creating an electronic resume or scannable resume, instead of using action verbs, you will want to use nouns that demonstrate specific skills and capabilities. For example, instead of using the word *managed*, use the keyword *management*. For more information on electronic (digital) resumes, see Chapter 7.

Accomplished
Achieved
Acquired
Acted as liaison
Adapted
Addressed
Administered
Advanced
Advised
Allocated
Analyzed
Appraised
Apprised
Approved
Arbitrated
Arranged
Assembled
Assigned
Audited
Augmented
Authored
Authorized
Awarded
Balanced
Boosted
Briefed
Broadened
Budgeted
Built
Calculated
Catalogued
Centralized

Chaired
Charted
Classified
Coached
Collected
Communicated
Communication skills
Compiled
Completed
Composed
Computed
Conceived
Conceptualized
Conducted
Consolidated
Consulted
Contacted
Contributed
Controlled
Coordinated
Counseled
Created
Critiqued
Cut
Decreased
Dedicated
Defined
Delegated
Delivered
Demonstrated
Designed
Determined

Developed

Devised

Diagnosed

Directed

Dispatched

Documented

Doubled

Downsized

Drafted

Edited

Educated

Eliminated

Enabled

Encouraged

Enforced

Engineered

Enhanced

Enlarged

Enlisted

Ensured

Established

Evaluated

Examined

Exceeded

Executed

Expanded

Expedited

Experienced

Explained

Facilitated

Fashioned

Focused

Forecasted

Formulated

Fostered

Founded

Generated

Grew

Guided

Handled

Headed up

Hired

Identified

Illustrated

Implemented

Improved

Increased

Influenced

Informed

Initiated

Innovated

Inspected

Inspired

Installed

Instigated

Instituted

Instructed

Integrated

Interpersonal skills

Interpreted

Interviewed

Introduced

Invented

Investigated

Launched

Lectured

Led

Licensed

Maintained

Managed

Marketed

Maximized

Measured

Mediated

Moderated

Monitored

Motivated

Navigated

Negotiated

Networked

Operated

Optimized

Organized

Originated

Overhauled

Oversaw

Performed

Persuaded

Planned

Prepared

Presented

Presided

Prioritized

Problem-Solving

Processed

Produced

Proficient in

Programmed

Projected

Promoted

Proposed

Provided

Publicized

Published

Purchased

Quadrupled

Ran

Realized

Recommended

Reconciled

Recorded

Recruited

Rectified

Reduced

Re-educated

Regulated

Remodeled

Repaired

Reported

Represented

Researched

Resolved

Responsible for

Restored

Restructured

Results oriented

Reviewed

Revitalized

Saved

Scheduled

Secured

Served as

Served on

Settled

Shaped

Skilled at

Sold

Solidified

Solved

Spearheaded

Specialized in

Specified

Stabilized

Stimulated

Streamlined

Strengthened

Structured

Successfully

Summarized

Supervised

Tabulated

Taught

Trained

Translated

Trimmed

Tripled

Unified

Updated

Upgraded

Upsized

Well versed

Wrote

APPENDIX B

defining and describing your job title

AS YOU WRITE your resume, it's critical that you properly communicate your past work experience in a way that readers easily understand. Never assume that the person reading your resume will totally comprehend your job responsibilities, accomplishments, and the skills needed to achieve your position's requirements, simply because you listed an impressive job title on your resume. Likewise, make sure the job titles you list under the employment section of your resume aren't too generic or so specific that they don't apply to another company's needs.

More often than not, someone's job title doesn't begin to describe anything about the job itself. For example, the job title *Manager* doesn't explain what the person's responsibilities were, whom they managed, what they managed, what they accomplished, what skills were required, or anything else a potential employer might find useful. This is all information potential employers need to know before they can make an educated decision about hiring you.

As you list your job titles, try to make them as descriptive as possible, so that someone who isn't necessarily familiar with your line of work will be able to determine what your strengths are as an applicant.

WHERE TO FIND INFORMATION ABOUT JOB RESPONSIBILITIES AND REQUIREMENTS

In addition to all of the online resources listed in Appendix C, the *Occupational Outlook Handbook* (http://www.bls.gov/oco) is a nationally recognized source of career information, designed to provide valuable assistance to individuals making decisions about their future work lives. This is an excellent resource for understanding job titles and responsibilities, and determining how you can incorporate this information into your resume.

For each job title or occupation featured within the *Occupational Outlook Handbook,* you will find detailed information about the:

- Nature of the work
- Working conditions
- Employment
- Training, other qualifications, and advancement
- Job outlook
- Earnings
- Related occupations
- Sources of additional information

From these sections, you should easily be able to find important buzzwords and other information to help you sell yourself to an employer. For example, if the *Occupational Outlook Handbook* lists specific qualifications required to land a job in the field or industry in which you hope to work, your resume should reflect that you have those qualifications (assuming you actually have them, of course).

Once you know a typical employer's requirements, you can cater your resume directly to a company by incorporating keywords, industry buzzwords, and other lingo that you know a potential employer is looking for. Pay careful attention to the "Training, Other Qualifications and Advancement" section of the entry in the *Occupational Outlook Handbook*. Here you will find a listing of specific skills, licenses, degrees, accreditations, and so forth required to enter a given field. Hopefully, your personal qualifications will match nicely with what the *Occupational Outlook Handbook* lists as required to land a job in the field in which you're interested.

READ HELP-WANTED ADS CAREFULLY

Another way to gather information that will help you list appropriate job titles, skills, and job-related responsibilities within your resume is to carefully read and evaluate the job description or help-wanted ad provided by the potential employer for which you'd like to work.

If the ad states the employer is looking for someone with three to five years' experience working in a specific position, make sure your resume reflects this information. Likewise, if the ad states proficiency using Microsoft Office 2000, for example, as a job requirement, this too needs to be highlighted in your resume.

Make sure the job opening being advertised is specifically the one you position yourself to be qualified to fill. Specific job titles, educational backgrounds, and skills listed on your resume should all match what the employer is looking for. In many cases, this requires that you customize your resume so that it's targeted to a specific job offered by a specific employer.

If the ad or job description to which you're responding doesn't contain enough detail, find five or ten others that are similar but from other employers. Try to incorporate the buzzwords and pertinent information from those ads into your resume to ensure your resume markets you as a qualified candidate for the type of job you're hoping to fill.

online career website directory and other online resources for job seekers

ON THE WORLD WIDE WEB, there are literally thousands of career-related websites. Some of these sites offer how-to advice about landing a job. Others offer a database of job listings that can be searched by region, industry, job type, salary, position, job title, or almost any other criteria. There are also resume databases allowing applicants to post their resume in hopes of it being read by a recruiter. If you need assistance creating your resume, there are professional resume writers who you can hire directly off the Web, many of whom also have informative websites of interest to job seekers.

The Web is an extremely powerful job-search tool that can not only help you find exciting job opportunities, but also research companies, network with other people in your field, and obtain valuable career-related advice.

Using any Internet search engine or portal, you can enter a keyword such as "resume," "job," "career," "job listings," or "help wanted" to find thousands of websites of interest to you. While Chapter 7 discusses how you can tap the power of the Internet in several different ways to help you find and land a job, the following is a listing of just some of the online resources available to you:

- 1st Resume Store   www.resumestore.com
- 1st Resumes   www.1stresumes.com
- 123-Jobs.com   www.123-jobs.com
- 10 Minute Resume   www.10minuteresume.com
- 6-Figure Jobs   www.6figurejobs.com
- ABA Résumé Writing   www.abastaff.com/career/resume/resume.htm
- About.com   jobsearch.about.com
- Accent Résumé Writing   www.accent-resume-writing.com/critiques
- Advanced Career Systems   www.resumesystems.com/career/Default.htm
- America's Employers   www.americasemployers.com
- America's Job Bank   www.ajb.dni.us
- auto resume   www.autoresume.com
- BestJobs USA   www.bestjobsusa.com
- Career City   www.careercity.com
- Career Creations   www.careercreations.com
- Career Express   www.careerxpress.com
- Career Management Services Corp.   www.getanewjob.com
- Career Resumes   www.career-resumes.com
- Career Station   www.careerstation.ca/resume_help.asp
- Career.com   www.career.com
- CareerBuilder   www.careerbuilder.com
- CareerMag   www.careermag.com
- CareerMosaic   www.careermosaic.com
- CareerNet   www.careers.org
- CareerPath   www.careerpath.com
- CareerShop   www.careershop.com
- CareerWeb   www.cweb.com

- College Central Network · · · · · · · · · · · · · www.employercentral.com
- College Grad.com · · · · · · · · · · · · · · · · · · · www.collegegrad.com
- Competitive Edge Career Service · · · · · www.acompetitiveedge.com
- Creative Keystrokes · · · · · · · · · · · · · · · · www.creativekeystrokes.com
- Creative Professional Resumes · · · · · · · www.resumesbycpr.com
- Curriculum Vitae Tips · · · · · · · · · · · · · · · www.cvtips.com
- Electronic Resume.com · · · · · · · · · · · · · · www.electronic-resume.com
- Employment Guide · · · · · · · · · · · · · · · · · · www.employmentguide.com
- eResumes · www.eresumes.com
- First Job: The Website · · · · · · · · · · · · · · · www.firstjob.com
- Gary Will's Worksearch · · · · · · · · · · · · · · www.garywill.com/worksearch
- Hot Jobs.com (Yahoo) · · · · · · · · · · · · · · · www.hotjobs.com
- JobBank USA · www.jobbankusa.com
- Job Hunting Tips · · · · · · · · · · · · · · · · · · · www.job-hunting-tips.com
- Job Island · www.jobisland.com
- JobLynx · www.joblynx.com
- JobNet.org · www.jobnet.org
- Jobs.com · www.jobs.com
- Job Search.com · www.jobsearch.com
- JobSource · www.jobsource.com
- Kforce.com · www.kforce.com
- Lighthouse Resumes · · · · · · · · · · · · · · · · www.lighthouseresumes.com
- Monster Resume Center · · · · · · · · · · · · · www.monster.com
- Medzilla.com · www.medzilla.com
- Professional Association of · · · · · · · · · · · www.parw.com
  Resume Writers & Career Coaches
- Proven Resumes · · · · · · · · · · · · · · · · · · · www.provenresumes.com
- Resume Office · www.resumeoffice.com
- Quintessential Careers · · · · · · · · · · · · · · www.quintcareers.com/resres.html
- Resumania · www.resumania.com
- Résumé-Magic · www.resume-magic.com
- Resume.com · www.resume.com
- resumedotcom · www.resumedotcom.com
- Salary.com · www.salary.com
- Taos Careers · www.taos.com/resumetips.html
- The Boston Herald's Job Find · · · · · · · · · www.jobfind.com

- tc resume   www.tcresume.com
- Ultimate Jobs   www.ultimatejobs.com
- Vault.com   www.vault.com/jobs/jobBoard/searchform.dsp
- WetFeet.com   www.wetfeet.com
- A Write Impression   www.awriteimpression.com
- Yahoo Careers   http://careers.yahoo.com

POPULAR WEB SEARCH ENGINES

To find additional online resources that can help you write your resume, find job opportunities, apply for jobs online, gather company or industry research, network with people in your field, or learn more about a specific profession, visit any of the popular Web search engines and choose keywords or search phrases you think will help you find the specific information for which you're looking.

Some of the popular search engines and information portals on the Web include:

- All-In-One Search   www.allonesearch.com
- AltaVista   www.altavista.co
- AOL   www.aol.com
- Ask Jeeves   www.ask.com
- Dogpile   www.dogpile.com
- Excite   www.excite.com
- Go.com   http://go.com
- Google   www.google.com
- Hotbot   www.hotbot.com
- Lycos   www.lycos.com
- MSN   search.msn.com
- Savvy Search   www.savvysearch.com
- Snap   www.snap.com
- Web Crawler   www.webcrawler.com
- Yahoo!   www.yahoo.com

Get the News You Need Online

When it comes to learning about industries, researching specific companies, or learning more about a job or profession, some of the most popular news-related websites that are ideal for research include:

- ABC News   www.abcnews.go.com
- Associated Press   www.ap.org
- Businesswire   www.businesswire.com
- CNN   www.cnn.com
- MSNBC   www.msnbc.com
- PR Newswire   www.prnewswire.com
- Reuters   www.reuters.com
- The Street   www.thestreet.com
- The Wall Street Journal   www.wsj.com
- USA Today   www.usatoday.com
- Yahoo News   dailynews.yahoo.com

A P P E N D I X D

print resources
for job seekers

IN ADDITION TO all of the resources available on the Web, there are a great number of career-related books that can help job seekers land the best possible job. If you can't find these books at your local bookstore, they're probably available online from Amazon.com (www.amazon.com) or Barnes and Noble Online (www.bn.com). CareerBookStore.com (www.careerbookstore.com) is another excellent resource for finding and purchasing career-related books online.

Also, consider reading the business and employment sections of your local, major daily newspaper.

CAREER-RELATED BOOKS

- *101 Best Cover Letters.* Jay A. Block and Michael Betrus. McGraw-Hill, 2000.
- *101 More Best Resumes.* Jay A. Block and Michael Betrus. McGraw-Hill, 2000.
- *101 Quick Tips for a Dynamite Resume.* Richard Fein. Impact Publications, 1998.
- *1500+ Keywords for $100,000+ Jobs.* Wendy S. Enelow. Impact Publications, 1998.
- *40-Minute Power Resume.* Beverly Hill. Renaissance Ink Press, 1999.
- *7-Minute Resumes.* Dana Morgan. ARCO, 2000.
- *Barrier-Breaking Resumes and Interviews.* Anita Doreen Diggs. Times Books, 1999.
- *Better Resumes in 3 Easy Steps.* Ben T. Field, Paul K. Wright. Delmar Publishing, 1999.
- *Can You Start Monday? A 9-Step Job Search Guide...Resume to Interview.* Cheryl A. Cage, ed. Cage Consulting, Inc., 1998.
- *The Complete Idiot's Guide to the Perfect Resume (3rd Edition).* Susan Ireland. Alpha Books, 2003.
- *The Complete Job-Search Handbook: Everything You Need to Know to Get the Job You Really Want.* Howard E. Figler. Owl Books, 1999.
- *The Complete Resume & Job Search for College Students.* Robert Lang Adams. Adams Media Corporation, 1999.
- *Cover Letters That Knock 'Em Dead (6th Edition).* Martin J. Yate. Adams Media Corporation, 2004.
- *Cyberspace Resume Kit: How to Make and Launch a Snazzy Online Resume.* Mary B. Nemnich and Fred Edmund Jandt. JIST Works, 1998.
- *Designing the Perfect Resume.* Pat Criscito. Barrons Educational Series, 2000.
- *The Easy Resume Guide: A Transferable Skills Approach.* Barbara J. Bowes. Hushion House, 1999.
- *The Edge Resume and Job Search Strategy.* G. Corbin et al. JIST Works, 2000.

- *The Elements of Resume Style: Essential Rules and Eye-Opening Advice for Writing Resumes and Cover Letters that Work.* Scott Bennett. AMACOM, 2005.
- *The Everything Get-A-Job Book: From Resume Writing to Interviewing to Finding Tons of Job Openings.* Steven Graber and Mark Lipsman, Compilers. Adams Media Corporation, 2000.
- *First Job, Great Job: America's Hottest Business Leaders Share Their Secrets.* Jason R. Rich. Authors Choice Press, 2000.
- *First Time Resume.* William McNeill. Adams Media Corporation, 2000.
- *From College to Career: Entry-Level Resumes for Any Major From Accounting to Zoology.* Donald Asher. Wet Feet Printing, 1999.
- *Gallery of Best Cover Letters: A Collection of Quality Cover Letters by Professional Resume Writers (2nd Edition).* David F. Noble. JIST Works, 2004.
- *Great Interview: Succesful Strategies for Getting Hired.* Vivian V. Eyre. LearningExpress, 2000.
- *Heart and Soul Resumes: 7 Never-Before-Published Secrets to Capturing Heart and Soul in Your Resume.* Chuck Cochran and Donna Peerce. Consulting Psychologists Press, 1998.
- *How to Figure Out, Once and for All, What You Really Want To Do With Your Life.* Darrell Daybre. The Center for Extraordinary Living, 1999.
- *Job Hunting for the Utterly Confused.* Jason R. Rich. McGraw-Hill, 1998.
- *Job Interviews That Get You Hired.* LearningExpress, 2006.
- *Job Searching Online for Dummies.* Pam Dixon. Wiley, 2000.
- *Job-Hunting on the Internet (4th Edition).* Richard Nelson Bolles. Ten Speed Press, 2005.
- *The Occupational Outlook Handbook: 2004–2005.* U.S. Department of Labor. JIST Works, 2000.
- *The Resume Handbook: How to Write Outstanding Resumes and Cover Letters for Every Situation.* Arthur D. Rosenberg and David Hizer. Adams Media Corporation, 2003.
- *Resume Magic: Trade Secrets of a Professional Resume Writer,* Susan Britton Whitcomb. JIST Works, 2003.
- *Resumes (Job Notes Series).* Timothy D. Haft. Princeton Review, 1997.

- *Resumes for Dummies (4th Edition)*. Joyce Lain Kennedy. Wiley, 2002.
- *Resumes That Knock 'Em Dead (6th Edition)*. Martin Yate. Adams Media, 2004.
- *Resumes That Mean Business (3rd Edition)*. David R. Eyler. Random House Reference, 1999.
- *Resumes (3rd Edition)*. Taunee S. Besson and Perri Capell. John Wiley & Sons, 1999.
- *The $100,000 Resume*. Craig Scott Rice. McGraw-Hill, 1998.
- *The Savvy Resume Writer: The Behavioral Advantage*. Ronald L. Krannich and Caryl Rae Krannich. Impact Publications, 1999.
- *The Unofficial Guide to Earning What You Deserve*. Jason R. Rich. Macmillan, 1999.
- *What Color Is Your Parachute? (2005 Edition)*. Richard Nelson Bolles. Ten Speed Press.

INDEX

OF EXHIBITS

sample resumes,
resume formats,
and tips on cover letters

I N D E X